BACK OF THE NET
100 Golden Goals

Bill Edgar has been a football writer for *The Times* since 1997 and also writes for various magazines. He co-wrote the book *A Football Fan's Guide to Europe* in 2009.

Roddy Murray is a freelance graphic artist and illustrator, now working primarily for *The Times*.

BACK OF THE NET
100 Golden Goals
Bill Edgar and Roddy Murray

Yellow Jersey Press
LONDON

INTRODUCTION

Spectacular goals are where it all starts. We all remember the golden goals of our youth – the glorious overhead kicks we saw on television and then discussed excitedly in the school playground, the extraordinary dribbles we tried to recreate in the back garden. As the years pass a debate begins – which are the greatest goals of all time?

When it comes to compiling a list of 100 great goals, as the saying goes, beauty is in the eye of the beholder. Were we right to pick Paul Gascoigne's free kick for Tottenham Hotspur against Arsenal in 1991 ahead of David Beckham's free kick for England against Greece in 2001? Was it justifiable to include neither of Arie Haan's long-range shots for Holland against West Germany and Italy at the 1978 World Cup and instead choose Chris Nicholl's 35-yard effort a year earlier for Aston Villa against Everton in the League Cup final?

Parameters had to be drawn. But having set these boundaries I tried to ignore the context of the match or the fame of the goal when making my selection. So a fine effort in a European Cup final would have less chance of making the list than a better strike in a routine league match. Well, I tried to do that – in the event one or two iconic goals were given a leg-up into the list.

Readers may note an apparent bias towards more recent times in the choice of goals. This is explained partly by the presence of television cameras now at all significant games, a modern development. The images of many great goals of the distant past live only in the memories of those who witnessed them in the flesh.

Another possible reason for the preponderance of modern goals – a contentious one – is that there are simply more of them now. Better pitches allow for smoother passing; improved fitness and diet mean greater athleticism and pace; and balls seem to swerve more, making long-range shots harder to save.

There will never be a consensus on the best 100 goals, but perhaps this list will encourage a few debates as to the merits of those I've included and those I've omitted. So take a look, enjoy 100 incredible moments in football, and see if you agree.

Bill Edgar

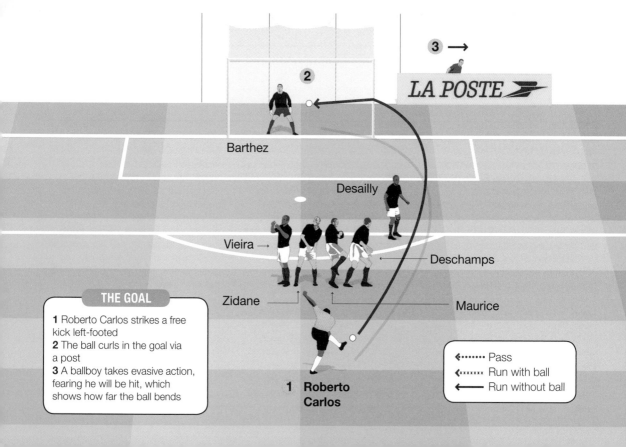

2

3 →

LA POSTE ⟫

Barthez

Desailly

Vieira →

← Deschamps

Zidane —

Maurice

THE GOAL

1 Roberto Carlos strikes a free kick left-footed
2 The ball curls in the goal via a post
3 A ballboy takes evasive action, fearing he will be hit, which shows how far the ball bends

1 Roberto Carlos

◀······· Pass
◀┄┄┄┄ Run with ball
◀───── Run without ball

001 ROBERTO CARLOS
France v Brazil, 3 June 1997
The inside-out swerve

The bravest footballers are those who volunteered to stand in the wall when Roberto Carlos was taking a free-kick. The strength of the Brazilian's shot had two roots: the speed at which he ran towards the ball, and his powerful thighs, or what he described as his "tree-trunk legs".

When this pace on the ball was allied with swerve and accuracy, it was almost impossible for a goalkeeper to stop. This was demonstrated in the opening match of a friendly tournament staged in 1997 by France as a practice for the following summer's World Cup. Poor Fabien Barthez, guarding the home side's goal, could only watch in bemusement.

The free-kick was awarded to Brazil 37 yards from goal in a central position and Roberto Carlos took a 10-yard run-up. The left-footed shot seemed to be heading so far to the right of goal that a ballboy crouched behind an advertising board flinched, but the ball bent dramatically inside the right-hand post.

Years later French physicists investigated the goal. The further a spinning ball travels, they said, the tighter the curve becomes, so the fact that Roberto Carlos shot from such a great distance explained the late movement. But the ferocity of the strike was also important, because it meant the ball was still travelling quickly enough as it approached the net to minimise the effect of gravity, allowing the fast spin to continue. But even if the free kick could be explained, no one has been able to repeat it. Not even Roberto Carlos.

"I'd practised in training but I've never seen a ball do what that one did. I had no idea how I did it. It was an impossible goal" **Roberto Carlos**

002 SAMIR NASRI
Arsenal v Porto, 9 March 2010
The zig-zag foray

THE MATCH

Champions League round of 16
Emirates Stadium

Arsenal 5
Bendtner 9, Bendtner 25, **Nasri 63**, Eboué 66, Bendtner pen 90
Porto 0
Att: 59,661

Arsène Wenger's impact at Arsenal was swift. In the manager's first eight full seasons at the club the team never finished outside the Premier League's top two and won four FA Cups. Then came the move to the new Emirates Stadium in 2006 and, year after year, trophies and the top two places in the league proved out of their reach.

Arsenal fans, though, had the consolation of knowing their team could, on their day, reach extremes of attacking beauty beyond any other English team. Their best players tended to be creative midfielders so, given Wenger's penchant for buying fellow Frenchmen, Samir Nasri was the perfect fit for the club.

Arsenal had not overturned a first-leg deficit in a European tie for more than 30 years when they hosted Porto in this match, having lost the away game 2–1, but that long sequence always seemed likely to end, especially as the Portuguese team had been beaten 4–0 at the Emirates Stadium the previous season. The third goal in this game gave Arsenal some breathing space but it also took the breath away.

Nasri had three opponents between him and the goal when he took possession near the right touchline and the trio surrounded him in a triangle after he had spun around Raul Meireles. But he jinked past Cristian Rodríguez and moved inside and then outside Álvaro Pereira before blasting a low shot into the far corner of the net. It was another treasure to compensate for the absence of trophies.

"He displayed amazing technique to weave through the defence"
Former Arsenal striker Ian Wright

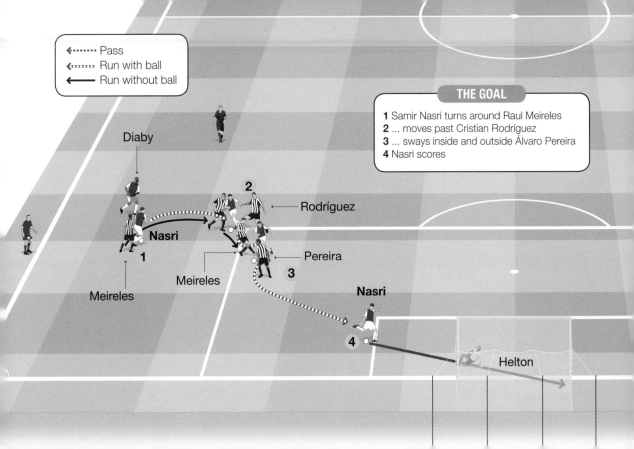

Pass

Run with ball

Run without ball

Diaby

THE GOAL

1 Samir Nasri turns around Raul Meireles
2 ... moves past Cristian Rodríguez
3 ... sways inside and outside Álvaro Pereira
4 Nasri scores

2

Rodríguez

Nasri

1

Pereira

3

Meireles

Meireles

Nasri

4

Helton

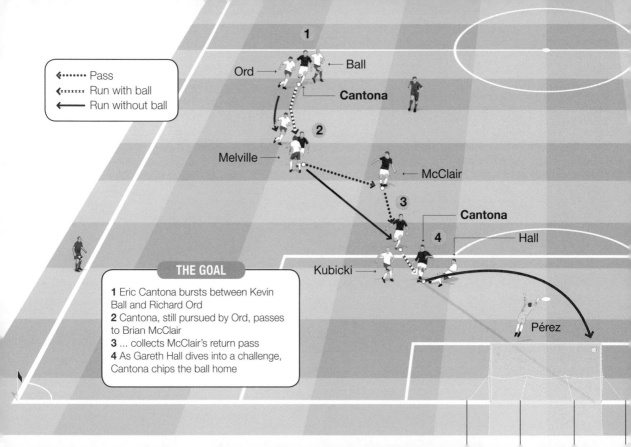

1

Ord → Ball

Cantona

◄······· Pass
◄∷∷∷∷∷ Run with ball
◄── Run without ball

2

Melville →

← McClair

3

Cantona

4

← Hall

Kubicki →

Pérez

THE GOAL

1 Eric Cantona bursts between Kevin
Ball and Richard Ord
2 Cantona, still pursued by Ord, passes
to Brian McClair
3 ... collects McClair's return pass
4 As Gareth Hall dives into a challenge,
Cantona chips the ball home

003 ERIC CANTONA
Manchester United v Sunderland, 21 December 1996
The slow-motion lob

He had insulted the France manager on television and members of a disciplinary panel to their faces, punched a team-mate, thrown the ball at the referee and kung-fu kicked a spectator. Eric Cantona was a maverick and he kept one shock in store until the end. The talisman for England's best team and still at his peak aged 30, he retired out of the blue in 1997.

Perhaps he feared the prospect of his standards falling in his thirties. He was accustomed to success, winning league titles with Marseille in 1991, Leeds United in 1992 and Manchester United in 1993, 1994, 1996 and 1997. The only missing link came in 1995, when he was suspended for the last four months of the season for that aforementioned attack on an abusive fan.

Five months from the end of his career United were struggling after two wins in eight games, which included defeats of 5–0 to Newcastle United and 6–3 to Southampton. Unusually they fielded three central defenders against Sunderland, but the abandonment of that cautious system after half an hour led to their flood of goals.

They saved the best till last. Cantona spun away from Kevin Ball and Richard Ord near the halfway line, exchanged passes with Brian McClair and shot so delicately that the ball seemed to take an age to reach the top-left corner of the net. The Frenchman, chest puffed out, turned 360 degrees to milk the applause of his adoring fans. He left them wanting more. They would continue to sing his name long after his premature retirement.

THE MATCH

English league
Old Trafford

Manchester United 5
Solskjaer 35, Cantona
pen 43, Solskjaer 48,
Butt 59, **Cantona 80**
Sunderland 0
Att: 55,081

"If I wasn't the opposition manager, I might say that goal was worth paying to see" **Sunderland manager Peter Reid**

004 CARLOS ALBERTO
Brazil v Italy, 21 June 1970
The blind-side blast

For many, Carlos Alberto's strike is the ultimate moment of footballing nostalgia: the greatest tournament's greatest goal. It had the perfect backdrop: the 1970 World Cup was the first televised in colour in Britain and many other countries, and the magical effect was amplified by the dazzling Mexican sun. Into this setting stepped Brazil in their bright yellow shirts, firing the imagination with skill, flair and recklessness in an age of negative and cynical football.

Brazil's six games produced 26 goals, many gifted by them to opponents through slack defending, and the final against Italy was typical. The South Americans led 3–1 with four minutes left but had no thoughts for playing out time cautiously.

Clodoaldo, unfazed by having teed up Italy's equaliser with a careless back-heel, embarked on a risky dribble in his own half in which he beat four Italians one by one. By jinking in the same direction each time he added to the sense of impudence. His circus act over, Clodoaldo slowed to a stroll and passed to Rivelino. Pace was injected into the move; then came another calm as Pelé, walking, stroked the ball nonchalantly to his right into the path of Carlos Alberto, arriving undetected from right back.

Carlos Alberto Torres, to give his full name, was more suited to attacking than defending, a trait of many subsequent Brazil full backs. Pelé spotted his captain's run and the quick-slow-quick-slow-quick move was complete as the ball was smashed home to give the World Cup a joyous final flourish.

"They seem to take it in turns to give an exhibition"
TV commentator Kenneth Wolstenholme

THE MATCH

**World Cup final
Aztec Stadium**

Brazil 4
Pelé 18, Gérson 66,
Jairzinho 71,
Carlos Alberto 86
Italy 1
Boninsegna 37
Att: 107,412

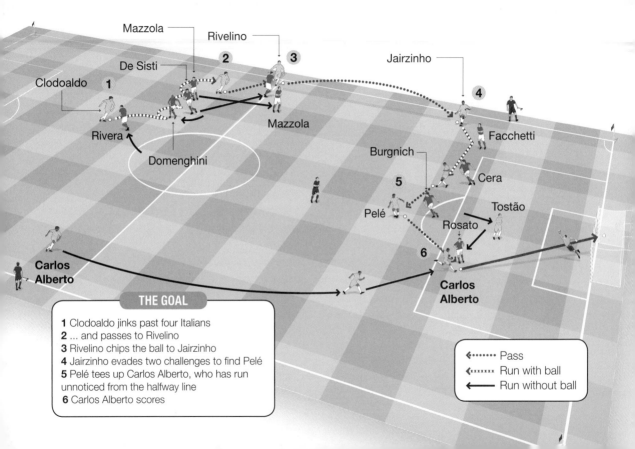

Mazzola

Rivelino

De Sisti

Clodoaldo **1**

2

3

Jairzinho

Rivera

Domenghini

Mazzola

4

Facchetti

Burgnich

Cera

5

Tostão

Pelé

Rosato

6

Carlos
Alberto

Carlos
Alberto

THE GOAL

1 Clodoaldo jinks past four Italians
2 ... and passes to Rivelino
3 Rivelino chips the ball to Jairzinho
4 Jairzinho evades two challenges to find Pelé
5 Pelé tees up Carlos Alberto, who has run
unnoticed from the halfway line
6 Carlos Alberto scores

◀······· Pass
◀┅┅┅┅ Run with ball
◀────── Run without ball

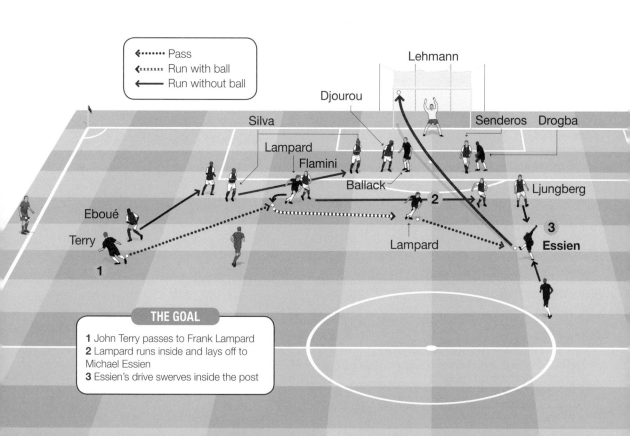

- - - - ▸ Pass
‧‧‧‧‧‧▸ Run with ball
——▸ Run without ball

Lehmann

Djourou

Silva

Lampard

Flamini

Ballack

Senderos   Drogba

Ljungberg

Eboué

Terry

1

Lampard

2

3
Essien

THE GOAL

1 John Terry passes to Frank Lampard
2 Lampard runs inside and lays off to
Michael Essien
3 Essien's drive swerves inside the post

005 MICHAEL ESSIEN
Chelsea v Arsenal, 10 December 2006
The drive around the bend

Just seven minutes remained of a breathless game when Frank Lampard sought out Michael Essien. Arsenal might have feared what would happen next, given the Ghanaian's nickname of the Bison. All power and stamina, the Chelsea player was still strong enough to sprint onto the ball and strike a ferocious equaliser from 30 yards before any opponent could react.

The goal earned a 1–1 draw and achieved the remarkable feat of deflecting attention away from Chelsea defender Ashley Cole, who had left Arsenal acrimoniously three months earlier. For much of the game Stamford Bridge had reverberated to the away fans' chants against "Cashley", who had talked of his anger at Arsenal's new contract offer to him of "only" £55,000 per week.

Cole's uncomfortable day worsened when Mathieu Flamini gave Arsenal the lead with 12 minutes left, but Chelsea were formidable on their own ground under José Mourinho, who avoided a home league defeat in his three years at the club. Substitute Arjen Robben's arrival helped turn the flow of play firmly in Chelsea's favour, but the team missed a hatful of chances.

It seemed as if Essien's scorching effort would feature among the catalogue of near misses when his shot initially headed wide of the goal. But the man who once claimed his boundless energy results from sleeping 14 hours a day saw the ball swerve inside the post and gave Chelsea fans a moment to dream about.

"One of the best, most unsaveable goals you will ever see"
TV analyst Alan Hansen

THE MATCH

English league
Stamford Bridge

Chelsea 1
Essien 84
Arsenal 1
Flamini 78
Att: 41,917

006 PETER BEARDSLEY
Liverpool v Nottingham Forest, 13 April 1988
The skip by the Kop

As Liverpool continued to extend what was already by far the most successful period of any club in English football history, some of their rivals would occasionally console themselves by claiming they possessed greater flamboyance than the Merseyside team. Even that crumb of comfort was denied them, though, when Kenny Dalglish built a side of irresistible entertainers at Anfield in the late 1980s.

Manchester United were among those claiming the moral high ground but two transfers in the summer of 1987 proved crucial. The Old Trafford club were offered John Barnes from Watford but they rejected the chance and Dalglish snapped him up; United did, in contrast, try to sign Peter Beardsley from Newcastle United but he also ended up at Liverpool, who now had two thrilling England forwards in their ranks.

The pair were to the fore as Liverpool avoided defeat in the first 29 league games, and they were already practically assured of a ninth league title in 13 seasons when they faced Nottingham Forest, their victims four days earlier in the FA Cup semi-finals.

If 1987–88 was Liverpool's most exhilarating year, this was the most breathtaking performance, with the fourth goal a joy to behold. Hemmed in by the corner flag, Barnes knocked the ball through Steve Chettle's legs, skipped over Gary Crosby's challenge and found Beardsley, who steered the ball home. That season Beardsley spoke of his pride that his team had become not only the best but the best to watch. There was no disagreement.

"One of the finest exhibitions of football I've ever seen"
Former England forward, Tom Finney

005 MICHAEL ESSIEN
Chelsea v Arsenal, 10 December 2006
The drive around the bend

Just seven minutes remained of a breathless game when Frank Lampard sought out Michael Essien. Arsenal might have feared what would happen next, given the Ghanaian's nickname of the Bison. All power and stamina, the Chelsea player was still strong enough to sprint onto the ball and strike a ferocious equaliser from 30 yards before any opponent could react.

The goal earned a 1–1 draw and achieved the remarkable feat of deflecting attention away from Chelsea defender Ashley Cole, who had left Arsenal acrimoniously three months earlier. For much of the game Stamford Bridge had reverberated to the away fans' chants against "Cashley", who had talked of his anger at Arsenal's new contract offer to him of "only" £55,000 per week.

Cole's uncomfortable day worsened when Mathieu Flamini gave Arsenal the lead with 12 minutes left, but Chelsea were formidable on their own ground under José Mourinho, who avoided a home league defeat in his three years at the club. Substitute Arjen Robben's arrival helped turn the flow of play firmly in Chelsea's favour, but the team missed a hatful of chances.

It seemed as if Essien's scorching effort would feature among the catalogue of near misses when his shot initially headed wide of the goal. But the man who once claimed his boundless energy results from sleeping 14 hours a day saw the ball swerve inside the post and gave Chelsea fans a moment to dream about.

THE MATCH

English league
Stamford Bridge

Chelsea 1
Essien 84
Arsenal 1
Flamini 78
Att: 41,917

"One of the best, most unsaveable goals you will ever see"
TV analyst Alan Hansen

006 PETER BEARDSLEY
Liverpool v Nottingham Forest, 13 April 1988
The skip by the Kop

As Liverpool continued to extend what was already by far the most successful period of any club in English football history, some of their rivals would occasionally console themselves by claiming they possessed greater flamboyance than the Merseyside team. Even that crumb of comfort was denied them, though, when Kenny Dalglish built a side of irresistible entertainers at Anfield in the late 1980s.

Manchester United were among those claiming the moral high ground but two transfers in the summer of 1987 proved crucial. The Old Trafford club were offered John Barnes from Watford but they rejected the chance and Dalglish snapped him up; United did, in contrast, try to sign Peter Beardsley from Newcastle United but he also ended up at Liverpool, who now had two thrilling England forwards in their ranks.

The pair were to the fore as Liverpool avoided defeat in the first 29 league games, and they were already practically assured of a ninth league title in 13 seasons when they faced Nottingham Forest, their victims four days earlier in the FA Cup semi-finals.

If 1987–88 was Liverpool's most exhilarating year, this was the most breathtaking performance, with the fourth goal a joy to behold. Hemmed in by the corner flag, Barnes knocked the ball through Steve Chettle's legs, skipped over Gary Crosby's challenge and found Beardsley, who steered the ball home. That season Beardsley spoke of his pride that his team had become not only the best but the best to watch. There was no disagreement.

THE MATCH

English league
Anfield

Liverpool 5
Houghton 18,
Aldridge 37, Gillespie 58,
Beardsley 79,
Aldridge 88
Nottingham Forest 0
Att: 39,535

"One of the finest exhibitions of football I've ever seen"
Former England forward, Tom Finney

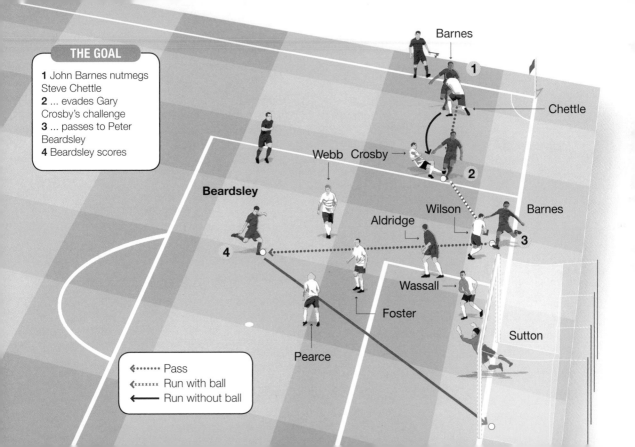

THE GOAL

1 John Barnes nutmegs Steve Chettle
2 ... evades Gary Crosby's challenge
3 ... passes to Peter Beardsley
4 Beardsley scores

Barnes

Chettle

Webb Crosby →

Beardsley

Aldridge →

Wilson →

Barnes

1

2

3

4

Wassall →

Foster

Sutton

Pearce

◄······· Pass
◄······· Run with ball
◄——— Run without ball

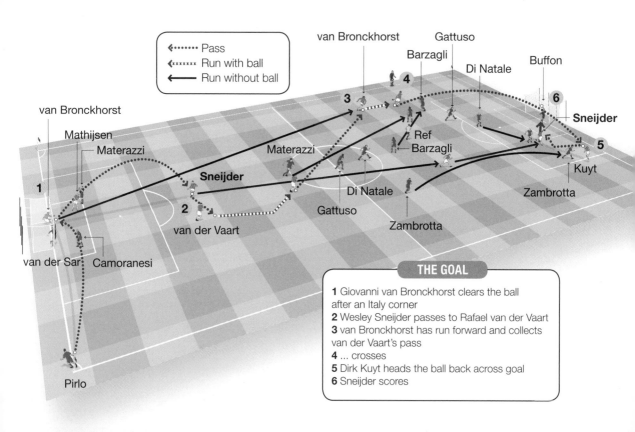

Pass
Run with ball
Run without ball

van Bronckhorst
Mathijsen
Materazzi
van Bronckhorst
Gattuso
Barzagli
Di Natale
Buffon
Sneijder
Ref
Barzagli
Materazzi
Sneijder
Di Natale
Kuyt
van der Vaart
Gattuso
Zambrotta
Zambrotta
van der Sar
Camoranesi
Pirlo

THE GOAL

1 Giovanni van Bronckhorst clears the ball after an Italy corner
2 Wesley Sneijder passes to Rafael van der Vaart
3 van Bronckhorst has run forward and collects van der Vaart's pass
4 ... crosses
5 Dirk Kuyt heads the ball back across goal
6 Sneijder scores

007 WESLEY SNEIJDER
Holland v Italy, 9 June 2008
The pitch-long counter attack

"It's better to create than destroy" was Holland coach Marco van Basten's philosophical message as he prepared to face Italy in his team's opening Euro 2008 game, maintaining his principles despite past events. He could doubtless recall an enterprising Dutch outfit losing a penalty shoot-out against the same opponents in the Euro 2000 semi-finals, having been unable to score against a side that retreated to blanket defence after suffering an early red card.

Italy were world champions so were expected to be formidable opponents in a strong group that also included France. But Holland had an inventive presence in Wesley Sneijder, who would be named man of the match on his 24th birthday after rounding off what was the ultimate counter-attacking goal to give his side a two-goal lead in Berne.

When Holland left-back Giovanni van Bronckhorst cleared a corner he was standing on his own goalline next to the far post, but 13 seconds later he was delivering a cross on the left edge of the Italy penalty area after the ball had been returned to him via Sneijder and Rafael van der Vaart. The cross was guided by Dirk Kuyt's head into the path of Sneijder, who hooked the ball home.

Such a brilliant move raised Dutch hopes of lifting the trophy, which were only increased by their subsequent 4–1 win over France. But, as with many previous Holland teams, they had flattered to deceive, and they lost tamely in the quarter-finals to Russia. Neutrals, though, would be grateful for van Basten's values.

THE MATCH

European championship group game
Stade de Suisse

Holland 3
van Nistelrooy 26,
Sneijder 31,
van Bronckhorst 79
Italy 0
Att: 30,777

"We played like a team and I think we have done the perfect job"
Wesley Sneijder

008 MATT LE TISSIER
Southampton v Newcastle United, 24 October 1993
The flick and flips

Kevin Keegan, the Newcastle United manager, was back at The Dell for the first time since his spell as a Southampton player ended 11 years earlier, but it was another comeback that interested home fans more. Matt Le Tissier, the team's entertainer and best player, had been dropped for the previous three games by Ian Branfoot and the forward was determined to show his manager what he had missed.

He certainly achieved that, scoring 23 of his side's remaining 38 league goals that season. To ram home the point, he produced two classic strikes on his return against Newcastle. For the second of those, the late winner, he controlled a pass on his thigh and hit an instant volley from outside the penalty area, but the first goal pipped it.

Le Tissier was dismayed by what he described as Branfoot's long-ball tactics, which he claimed took the fun out of playing. On this occasion, the goal did indeed start with a long punt upfield that Iain Dowie headed down, but there was nothing ugly about what followed. Le Tissier controlled the ball with the side of his boot as it dropped behind him, and then flicked it past Barry Venison and chipped it over Kevin Scott.

The nature of the shot, a mishit, did not detract from the skills he had displayed in the build-up. Le Tissier had enjoyed the last laugh over his manager and would do so in the long term, too. Branfoot was sacked three months later but Le Tissier thrilled Southampton fans for another eight years.

"I just had an unbelievable feeling inside me that I could do anything" Matt Le Tissier

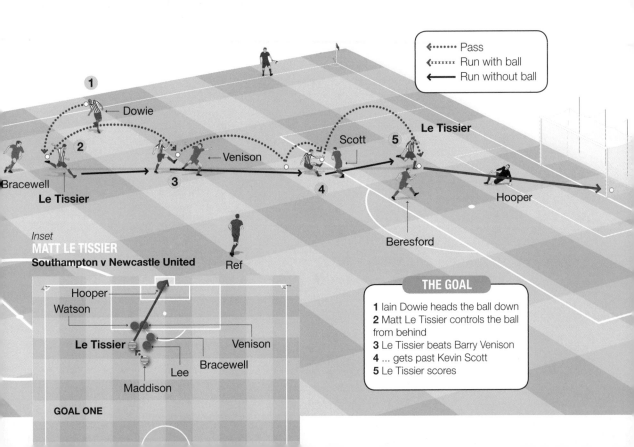

Pass
Run with ball
Run without ball

① Dowie
② Le Tissier
Bracewell
Le Tissier
3 Venison
4 Scott 5 **Le Tissier**
Hooper
Beresford

Inset
MATT LE TISSIER
Southampton v Newcastle United
Ref

Hooper
Watson
Le Tissier
Venison
Lee Bracewell
Maddison

GOAL ONE

THE GOAL

1 Iain Dowie heads the ball down
2 Matt Le Tissier controls the ball from behind
3 Le Tissier beats Barry Venison
4 ... gets past Kevin Scott
5 Le Tissier scores

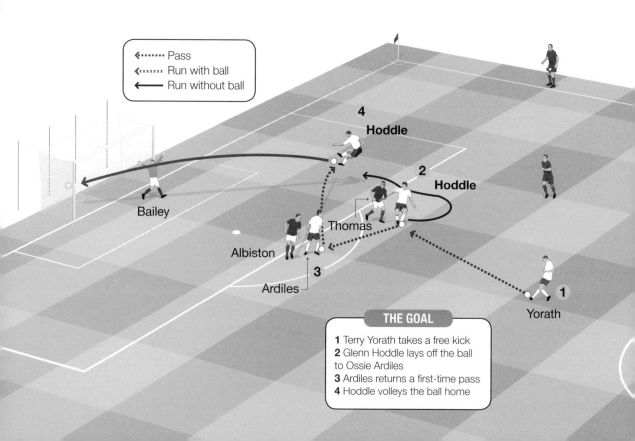

Pass
Run with ball
Run without ball

4
Hoddle

2
Hoddle

Bailey

Thomas

Albiston

3

Ardiles

Yorath
1

THE GOAL

1 Terry Yorath takes a free kick
2 Glenn Hoddle lays off the ball
to Ossie Ardiles
3 Ardiles returns a first-time pass
4 Hoddle volleys the ball home

009 GLENN HODDLE
Tottenham Hotspur v Manchester United,
29 August 1979 The high-jump hit

When Tottenham lost their goalkeeper to injury during an FA Cup replay away to Manchester United in January 1980 Glenn Hoddle, a midfielder, went in goal and held out for more than an hour as his side won 1–0 after extra-time. Earlier in the season he had made another striking contribution – albeit more conventional – against the same opponents in the League Cup.

Whereas English footballers are characterised by energy and aggression more than technique, Hoddle was the opposite. Often accused of strolling through games, he could hit a 50-yard pass accurately with either foot or control one from a team-mate in an instant. Having gained a stone and a half in the previous 18 months, his perfectly timed shots now packed greater power.

Hoddle possessed a team-mate of similar ingenuity and talent in the Argentine Ossie Ardiles, and the pair combined brilliantly here. The Englishman flicked the ball to his colleague, spun around Mickey Thomas and ran onto the return pass. Without letting the ball bounce, he leapt high to execute an exquisite volley into the far corner of the net.

Although Tottenham lost the second-leg 3–1 to exit the competition, this goal in the first game proved significant for the 21-year-old Hoddle as it brought his talent closer to the spotlight. Three months later he made his England debut against Bulgaria, and his fine display then, which included another excellent goal, heralded the start of a long international career.

"My heaven they really got their talent together then"
TV commentator Barry Davies

010 GEORGI KINKLADZE
Manchester City v Southampton, 16 March 1996
The ball on a string

When he first arrived at Manchester City in 1995 Georgi Kinkladze's homesickness prompted his mother to bring him his favourite food from his native Georgia. But eventually he settled so well that, despite being considered a world-class player, he remained at City after their relegation and even stayed to the bitter end of the campaign in which they were consigned to the third tier.

City fans had a further reason to be grateful to Khatuna Kinkladze beyond helping her son to acclimatise. The ballet lessons she insisted he attend as a boy helped give him the strength, balance and lightness of foot to produce his famous dribbles past opponents. None is better remembered than his effort for City against a Southampton team who were rivals in the battle to stay in the Premier League in 1996.

Five minutes earlier Kinkladze had tapped home the opening goal but this was a different matter entirely. Running as if the ball was tied to his left foot, he cut in from the right touchline, jinked inside Simon Charlton, evaded David Hughes, slipped past Ken Monkou, stepped over the sliding Hughes and dinked the ball over Dave Beasant.

City's supporters went wild and no wonder. Any goal – let alone a classic such as this – was a cause for great celebration in a season when their team were the Premier League's lowest scorers. That lack of attacking potency proved their downfall but Kinkladze stayed at City, leaving English football with the incongruity of his brilliance on display down in the second tier.

"As close to that famous Maradona goal against England as you could see" Manchester City manager Alan Ball

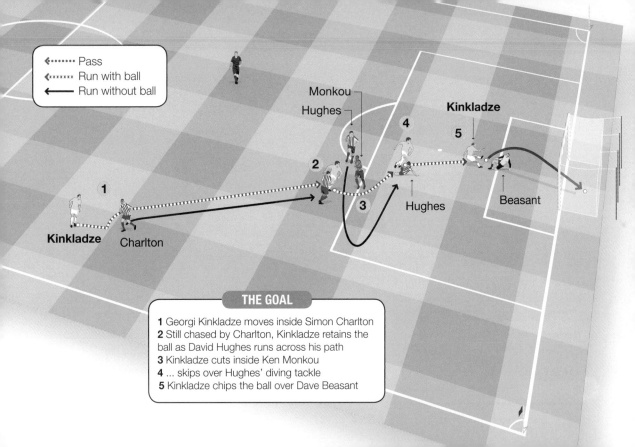

Pass
Run with ball
Run without ball

Monkou
Hughes

Kinkladze

4

5

2

3

Hughes

1

Beasant

Kinkladze   Charlton

THE GOAL

1 Georgi Kinkladze moves inside Simon Charlton
2 Still chased by Charlton, Kinkladze retains the
ball as David Hughes runs across his path
3 Kinkladze cuts inside Ken Monkou
4 ... skips over Hughes' diving tackle
5 Kinkladze chips the ball over Dave Beasant

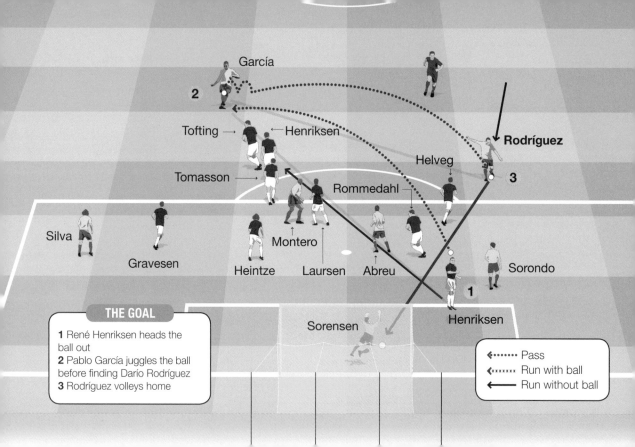

García

2

Tofting →   ← Henriksen

Tomasson →

Rodríguez

Helveg

Rommedahl

3

Silva

Montero

Gravesen

Heintze   Laursen   Abreu

Sorondo

THE GOAL

1 René Henriksen heads the ball out
2 Pablo García juggles the ball before finding Darío Rodríguez
3 Rodríguez volleys home

Sorensen

Henriksen   **1**

◀······· Pass
◀:::::::: Run with ball
◀——— Run without ball

011 DARÍO RODRÍGUEZ
Uruguay v Denmark, 1 June 2002
The keepy-uppy and whack

Uruguay won the first two World Cups they entered, in 1930 and 1950, but in subsequent tournaments the lasting impression they left was of a team that mixed the boring with the brutal. They favoured defence and the only kind of attacking they seemed to produce involved physically assaulting the opposition. Those expecting a repeat of such behaviour in 2002, however, were pleasantly surprised.

Having lost 6–1 to Denmark at the 1986 World Cup, Uruguay might have considered adopting their traditional caution when meeting the same opponents 16 years later in South Korea, but they played freely and conjured up arguably the tournament's best goal for good measure. It came from Darío Rodríguez, who, well built and tall for a full back, possessed a powerful shot.

Pablo García also takes great credit for the goal, which stemmed from a Uruguay corner. The midfielder stood just outside the Denmark penalty area as he controlled a clearance on the volley, then tapped the ball up again to draw opponents towards him and away from Rodríguez. Finally García knocked a pass diagonally forward to his team-mate, who had the space to drive his shot into the top corner. The ball had not touched the ground since the corner was taken.

Sadly for Uruguay they lost the match and did not reach the group stage. They also missed the next tournament after Rodríguez missed a penalty in a play-off shoot-out defeat by Australia. At least he has this scintillating goal as a warm World Cup memory.

"Did [goalkeeper Thomas] Sorensen see it? I doubt it"
TV commentator Peter Drury

012 LEON OSMAN
Everton v Larissa, 25 October 2007
The breathtaking break

After the rage, the rejuvenation. Everton's weekend had been ruined by a controversial 2–1 defeat to city rivals Liverpool in which they'd suffered two red cards and were denied a clear penalty, but their frustrations with officialdom were forgotten as they produced an exhilarating goal on their return to action.

Everton's manager David Moyes had often mentioned his team's lack of height as a problem, but here he was grateful for the agility and fleet-footedness of a quartet of players whose average height was 5ft 8in. Tim Cahill, Leighton Baines, Steven Pienaar and Leon Osman combined in a blur to leave their Greek opponents chasing shadows.

Cahill, perhaps Everton's best player, was restored to the line-up after seven months out with a broken metatarsal and he launched the move by bursting past a defender on the halfway line and sending Baines clear on the left. The defender did not break stride as he played the ball first-time inside to Pienaar, who also delivered an instant pass, an inspired back flick into Osman's path.

Taking his cue from his team-mates, Osman did not wait to control the ball. Instead he thrashed a shot that initially headed outside the post but then swung back inside.

This was Everton's opening game in their UEFA Cup group, a stage they had reached by recording their first victory in a European tie for 12 years. It was already a significant fixture – this goal merely added to the history.

"This was the Blues at their slick, quick and unplayable best"
Dominic King, *Liverpool Echo*

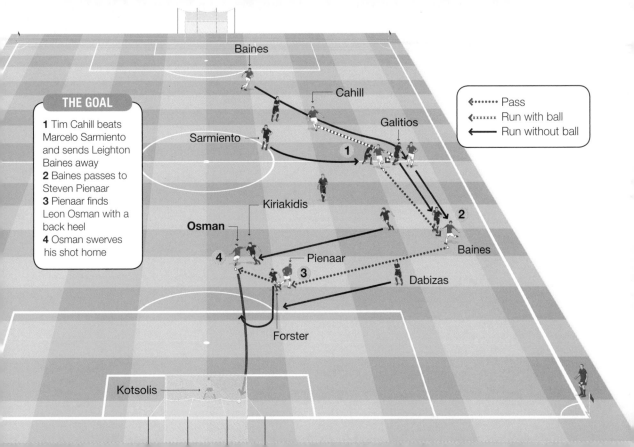

Baines

Cahill

Galitios

THE GOAL

1 Tim Cahill beats
Marcelo Sarmiento
and sends Leighton
Baines away
2 Baines passes to
Steven Pienaar
3 Pienaar finds
Leon Osman with a
back heel
4 Osman swerves
his shot home

Sarmiento

◀┈┈┈┈ Pass
◀┈┈┈┈ Run with ball
◀━━━ Run without ball

1

2

Kiriakidis

Osman

Baines

4

Pienaar

3

Dabizas

Forster

Kotsolis

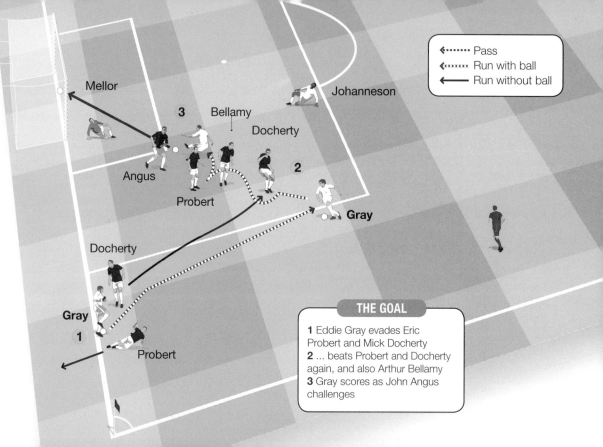

Mellor

3

Bellamy

Docherty

Johanneson

Angus

Probert

Docherty

Gray

Gray

1

Probert

Pass

Run with ball

Run without ball

THE GOAL

1 Eddie Gray evades Eric Probert and Mick Docherty
2 ... beats Probert and Docherty again, and also Arthur Bellamy
3 Gray scores as John Angus challenges

013 EDDIE GRAY
Leeds United v Burnley, 4 April 1970
The drag-back display

Eddie Gray required more than just skill to hold the ball for 13 seconds – an age in football terms – as he dribbled past the Burnley defence to score his remarkable goal. The Leeds United winger needed enormous stamina simply to avoid collapsing in the Turf Moor mud, given his club's recent punishing schedule as they chased a treble.

Over the previous two weeks, the Scot had played on Saturday (v Wolverhampton Wanderers, league), Monday (v Manchester United, FA Cup semi-final replay), Thursday (v Manchester United, FA Cup semi-final, second replay), Saturday (v Southampton, league), Wednesday (v Celtic, European Cup semi-final, first-leg) and Thursday (v West Ham United, league). Two days later he was back facing Burnley yet he was still able to produce two memorable goals.

First Gray opened the scoring with a precise chip from about 35 yards that just cleared the goalkeeper's head. Then, with the scores level, came the masterpiece. As Leeds' Albert Johanneson lay injured on the ground nearby, Gray acted alone, moving away from two opponents on the byline and slaloming past three in the penalty area before stabbing the ball home.

Leeds, who had even fitted in an eighth game in that crazy 15-day period (a league game against Derby County without Gray) could not handle the strain. They lost to Celtic in the European Cup semi-finals and to Chelsea in an FA Cup Final replay, while finishing second behind Everton in the league. Gray's genius had gone unrewarded.

THE MATCH

English league
Elland Road

Leeds United 2
Gray 6, Gray 71
Burnley 1
Faulkner og 25
Att: 24,691

"One of the best goals I've seen since Eddie scored in 1966. He beat eight men then. Today he only beat six" Leeds manager Don Revie

014 GEORGE WEAH
AC Milan v Verona, 8 September 1996
The pitch-length meander

THE MATCH

**Italian league
San Siro**

AC Milan 4
Simone 49, Simone 66,
Weah 86, Baggio 90
Verona 1
de Vitis 25
Att: 50,000

AC Milan had already agreed in principle to George Weah's transfer from Paris St-Germain when the two teams met in the Champions League semi-finals in 1995. The striker, perhaps anxious with such a prestigious move in the offing, played so poorly that the Italian club tried to drop the deal. But eventually they pushed ahead and signed him as planned, to their subsequent relief.

The desire of Weah, a Liberian, to join one of the world's leading clubs was understandable given that his country's lack of footballing strength meant he held no realistic hopes of enjoying success at international level. His standing as a player at home was so great – as was his wealth from playing in Europe – that when his country was hit by civil war he funded and arranged for the national team's home qualifiers for the 1998 World Cup to be staged in Ghana.

In the year he joined Milan he became the first African to win the European Player of the Year award, which was open to anyone playing in Europe, and was also named FIFA World Player of the Year. The reason for such accolades was underlined on the opening day of the 1996–97 season.

When a Verona corner was overhit, Weah gathered the ball at the far side of the penalty area and ran … and ran. Around 90 yards later, after holding off three challenges, he slid the ball home.

Milan would go on to have a dreadful season – their worst for 15 years – but, while Weah was shining on that sunny September afternoon, their fans could still dream.

"What made it a great goal wasn't the run, it was the beautiful finish" George Weah

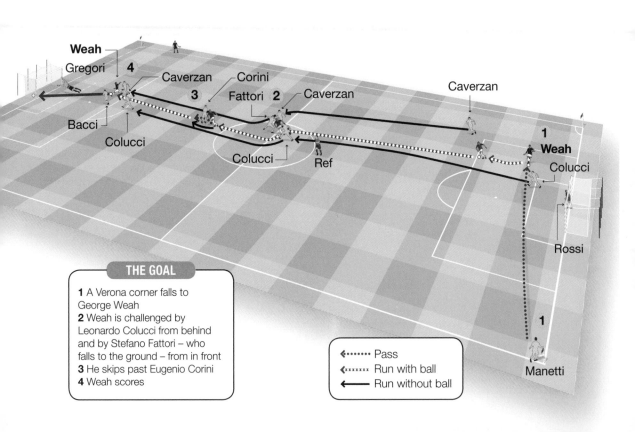

Weah
Gregori
4
Caverzan — Corini
3
Fattori **2**
Caverzan
Caverzan
1
Weah
Colucci
Bacci
Colucci
Colucci
Ref
Rossi
1

THE GOAL

1 A Verona corner falls to George Weah
2 Weah is challenged by Leonardo Colucci from behind and by Stefano Fattori – who falls to the ground – from in front
3 He skips past Eugenio Corini
4 Weah scores

Manetti

•••••• Pass
••••••• Run with ball
⟵ Run without ball

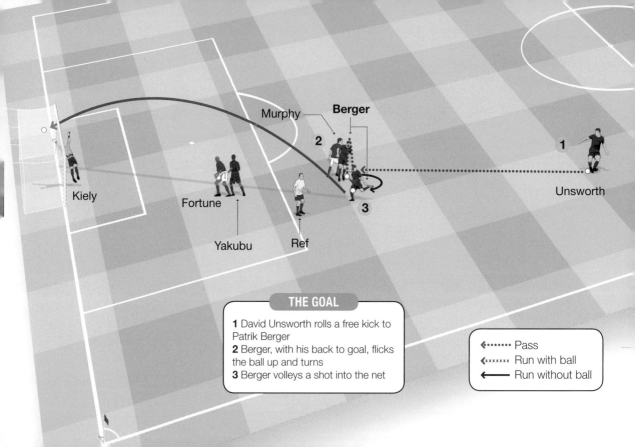

Murphy

Berger

2

Kiely

Fortune

Yakubu

Ref

3

1

Unsworth

THE GOAL

1 David Unsworth rolls a free kick to Patrik Berger

2 Berger, with his back to goal, flicks the ball up and turns

3 Berger volleys a shot into the net

◀········ Pass

◀:::::::: Run with ball

◀——— Run without ball

015 PATRIK BERGER
Charlton Athletic v Portsmouth, 21 August 2004
The swivel and swipe

Three minutes remained when Jonathan Fortune's free-kick for Charlton Athletic skimmed the head of Portsmouth defender David Unsworth and floated gently towards Shaka Hislop, the goalkeeper. Many spectators' eyes had already turned away because it was inconceivable that Hislop would not gather the ball and seek out a team-mate – except that he allowed it to squeeze under his body and into the goal.

The resulting defeat was a blow for Portsmouth but also a shame for Patrik Berger, their midfielder, whose extraordinary goal now counted for nothing. Oddly, exactly the same would happen the following season, when Andrés D'Alessandro (see goal 041) also scored a brilliant long-range goal with his left foot for Portsmouth in another 2–1 defeat away to Charlton.

Berger's career revolved around England. He rose to prominence helping the Czech Republic reach the Euro '96 final at Wembley. This helped earn him a move to Liverpool shortly afterwards and he stayed in the country for twelve years, seven of which were spent at Anfield before he joined Portsmouth on a free transfer as his injuries became more frequent.

He was reminded of his former club when he received the ball from Unsworth with his back to goal about 30 yards out. He was marked tightly by his former Liverpool team-mate Danny Murphy, but a flick of the ball earned a yard of space and he turned, smashing a volley over Dean Kiely's head. Sadly, the game's other goalkeeper would take the gloss off Berger's day.

"That was a fantastic strike – you won't see many better than that"
Charlton manager Alan Curbishley

016 DENNIS BERGKAMP
Holland v Argentina, 4 July 1998
The freakish control

Dennis Bergkamp was known as "The Iceman" and twice in 1997–98 he showed why. Each time, with his team chasing a late winning goal, he remained unflustered to trap a long pass dead in the penalty area, evade the attentions of a defender close by and score. These strikes came near the start and end of a season in which he won both of English football's main awards for player of the year.

His first goal came during an astonishing finish to Arsenal's Premier League game away to Leicester City. After the home side completed a late comeback to draw level at 2–2 in stoppage time, David Platt's chip forward was controlled on the volley by Bergkamp, who flicked up the ball to skirt round Matt Elliott and side-footed it home to complete his hat-trick. Yet, incredibly, Steve Walsh, the Leicester defender, found time to make the final score 3–3.

If this goal has been overshadowed a little by the game's many sub-plots, Bergkamp's effort for Holland in Marseille retains a clear place in World Cup history. He brought down Frank de Boer's 60-yard pass, cut inside Roberto Ayala and jabbed the ball into the net. His 36th goal for Holland, which broke the record, gained revenge for his country's defeat by Argentina in the 1978 final.

This World Cup, in which Holland fell to Brazil in the semi-finals, would be Bergkamp's last because his fear of flying precluded his involvement in Japan and South Korea in 2002. At least he could pluck a ball out of the sky.

"You can't imagine a goal like that. It just happens"
Dennis Bergkamp

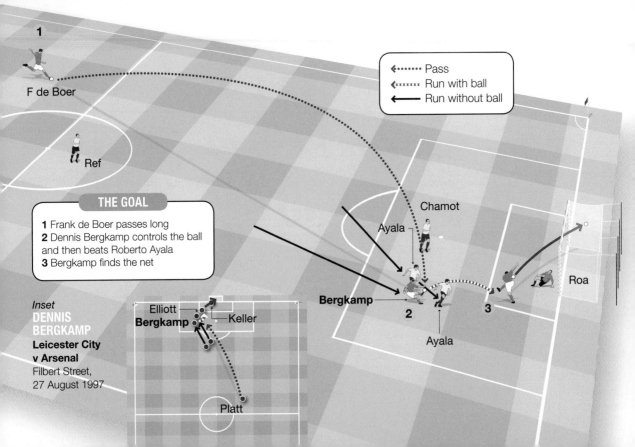

1

F de Boer

Ref

←······· Pass
←≡≡≡≡≡ Run with ball
←——— Run without ball

THE GOAL

1 Frank de Boer passes long
2 Dennis Bergkamp controls the ball and then beats Roberto Ayala
3 Bergkamp finds the net

Inset
DENNIS BERGKAMP
Leicester City v Arsenal
Filbert Street,
27 August 1997

Elliott
Bergkamp
Keller
Platt

Chamot
Ayala
Bergkamp
2
Ayala
3
Roa

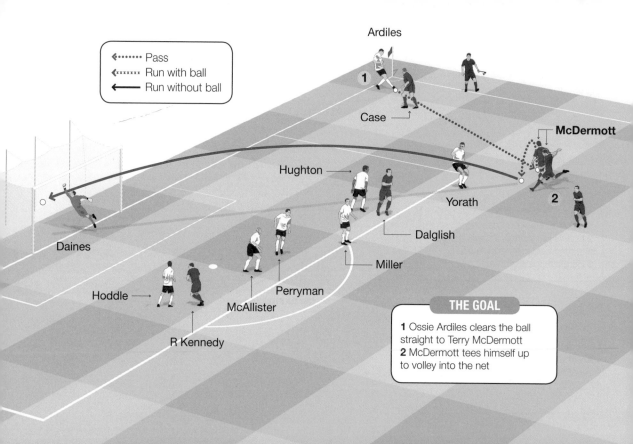

Pass
Run with ball
Run without ball

Ardiles

1

Case

McDermott

Hughton

Yorath

Dalglish

2

Miller

Daines

Hoddle

Perryman

McAllister

R Kennedy

THE GOAL

1 Ossie Ardiles clears the ball
straight to Terry McDermott
2 McDermott tees himself up
to volley into the net

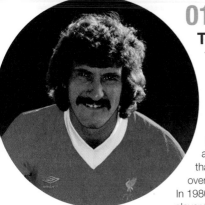

017 TERRY MCDERMOTT
Tottenham Hotspur v Liverpool, 8 March 1980
The wallop from out wide

There was little doubt over Liverpool's strongest XI in 1979–80. The starting line-up for this match was exactly the same as for 24 of their 42 league games that season, a remarkably high figure. But within that XI there also seemed little doubt over who was the best player at the time. In 1980 Terry McDermott became the first player to win both of English football's two main player of the year awards, hailed by players and journalists alike.

McDermott enjoyed a fine goalscoring record for a midfielder during his trophy-laden eight years at Anfield and many of his strikes were spectacular. One such goal was scored here, and it also proved vital because it was all Liverpool had to show for their dominance of this FA Cup quarter-final.

He needed help, though, from Ossie Ardiles, Tottenham's Argentine, whose desperation to play in the final was immortalised in a song before the 1981 FA Cup climax ("Ossie's going to Wembley, his knees have gone all trembly"). Perhaps it was nerves that led him to clear the ball gently and directly to McDermott.

The England international, standing a few yards away from the right-hand corner of the penalty area, chipped the ball up for himself to send a dipping volley into the far corner of the net beyond Tottenham goalkeeper Barry Daines. Yet Liverpool lost to Arsenal in the next round and McDermott would never add the FA Cup to his series of league, European Cup and League Cup triumphs with the club. At least Ardiles – a year later – achieved that.

"It took Barry Daines of Tottenham by surprise, but what can you do with a shot like that" TV commentator John Motson

018 WAYNE ROONEY
Everton v Arsenal, 19 October 2002
The upward curve

The climax to this match produced an historic "I was there" moment for the crowd to reminisce about, except that Bill Kenwright wasn't there. The Everton owner must curse the fact that another appointment forced him to leave Goodison Park before Wayne Rooney's late winning goal. Still, he would have been thrilled that a player whose great potential had been discussed for months had shown he possessed a temperament for the big occasion.

Everton fans, whose number included Kenwright and Rooney themselves, might have feared the worst at kick-off: Arsenal had achieved the league and FA Cup double the previous season and were unbeaten in 30 league games, 25 of which were victories.

Everton's task was made harder when Arsenal scored for a record 49th league game in a row – the previous best was Chesterfield's 46 – but they were level by the time Rooney emerged as a substitute with ten minutes left. Five days short of his 17th birthday, he controlled Thomas Gravesen's 90th-minute lofted pass and curled home a shot off the underside of the crossbar past David Seaman, a goalkeeper who was 22 years his senior.

Rooney was thus the youngest goalscorer in the Premier League's ten-year history and four months later he would become England's youngest ever player. Arsenal's Thierry Henry sought him out at the final whistle to shake his hand. He could recognise a fellow great striker when he saw one.

"At 16 Rooney is already a complete footballer"
Arsenal manager Arsène Wenger

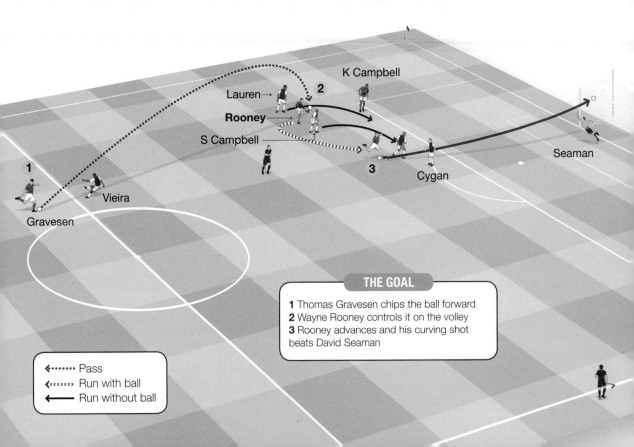

K Campbell

Lauren →

2

Rooney →

S Campbell →

3

Cygan

Seaman

1

Vieira

Gravesen

THE GOAL

1 Thomas Gravesen chips the ball forward
2 Wayne Rooney controls it on the volley
3 Rooney advances and his curving shot beats David Seaman

�..... Pass
⬅:::::: Run with ball
⬅—— Run without ball

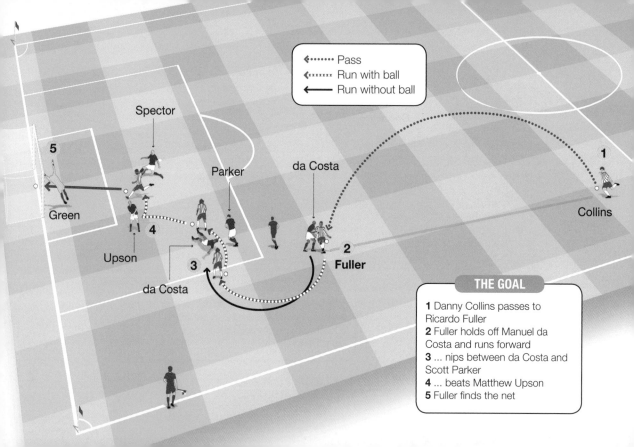

Pass
Run with ball
Run without ball

Spector

Parker

da Costa

Collins

1

Green

5

Upson

4

3

da Costa

2
Fuller

THE GOAL

1 Danny Collins passes to Ricardo Fuller
2 Fuller holds off Manuel da Costa and runs forward
3 ... nips between da Costa and Scott Parker
4 ... beats Matthew Upson
5 Fuller finds the net

019 RICARDO FULLER
West Ham United v Stoke City, 27 March 2010
The snaking trail

The omens hardly favoured Ricardo Fuller as he left the Stoke City bench in the 67th minute. He had spent most of the previous week at home with a stomach bug (hence his demotion to substitute) and on his previous visit to Upton Park, a year earlier, he had been sent off for punching Andy Griffin, his own captain, in an argument over a West Ham United goal.

Yet, just two minutes after his introduction, he scored a remarkable solo effort. After holding off Manuel da Costa to control Danny Collins' looped pass, Fuller burst between the defender and Scott Parker, jinked inside Matthew Upson and beat goalkeeper Robert Green. In a flash the game had been decided.

The origin of the goal might have raised a wry smile among Stoke fans. The home side had been obsessed by Stoke throw-ins, so much so that they had erected advertising hoardings closer to the pitch than normal to try to lessen the impact of Rory Delap's long throw-ins by denying him a proper run-up. Yet it was one of their own throw-ins that fell at Collins' feet and led to the goal. Fuller's strike inflicted their sixth consecutive league defeat.

Having played for seven teams in five years before joining Stoke in 2006, the Jamaican striker had finally found a club where he could settle properly, not withstanding the public disagreement with his team-mate in the previous season. If Stoke played their part in helping Fuller to feel at home, they were rewarded handsomely on this occasion.

"He is so strong and his feet are so quick. It was a special goal"
Tony Pulis, Stoke manager

020 JOHN HARKES
Derby County v Sheffield Wednesday,
12 December 1990 The clout from the right

At the 1990 World Cup Peter Shilton helped England reach the semi-finals and concluded his international career on 125 caps, a record for his country. At the same tournament, in stark contrast, John Harkes played in the United States' three group matches and lost them all. But when the two players faced each other on the pitch later that year it was the American who enjoyed the better of the occasion.

Harkes had only made his debut in the English game six weeks earlier having left his homeland to play professionally. On arrival he encountered hostility among fans of his club, Sheffield Wednesday: the sentiment, said the player, was that he should stick to American sports. But his popularity soon improved, particularly when he scored a spectacular goal against Derby County.

Harkes had advanced from his right-back position when he collected a crossfield pass from Nigel Worthington. The American carried the ball forward and fired a shot from 35 yards that was still rising as it hit the roof of the net. Shilton, the Derby goalkeeper, was only halfway through his dive as the ball flashed past him.

Derby were one of four top-division victims for Wednesday – a second-tier club – in what was to prove a triumphant League Cup campaign. After this came victories away to Coventry City, at home and away against Chelsea in the semi-finals and against Manchester United in the final. They also gained promotion. Derby certainly didn't forget Harkes' goal – they signed him three years later.

"That was the breakthrough. The next game at home the fans had come over to John's side" John Harkes' wife, Cindy

THE MATCH

**League Cup fourth round replay
Baseball Ground**

Derby County 1
Micklewhite 59
Sheffield Wednesday 2
Harkes 33, Williams 52
Att: 17,050

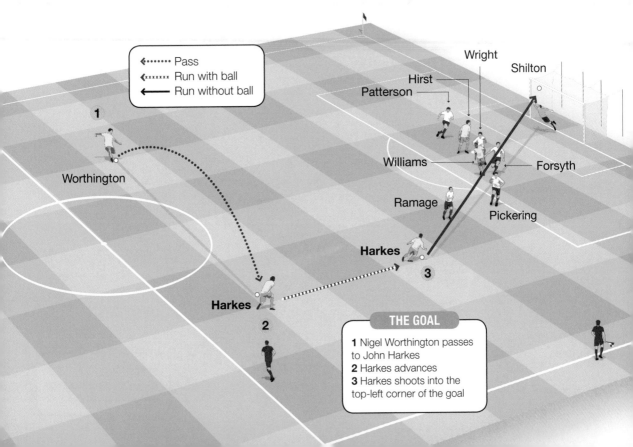

Pass

Run with ball

Run without ball

Wright

Shilton

Hirst

Patterson

1

Williams

Forsyth

Worthington

Ramage

Pickering

Harkes

Harkes

3

2

THE GOAL

1 Nigel Worthington passes to John Harkes

2 Harkes advances

3 Harkes shoots into the top-left corner of the goal

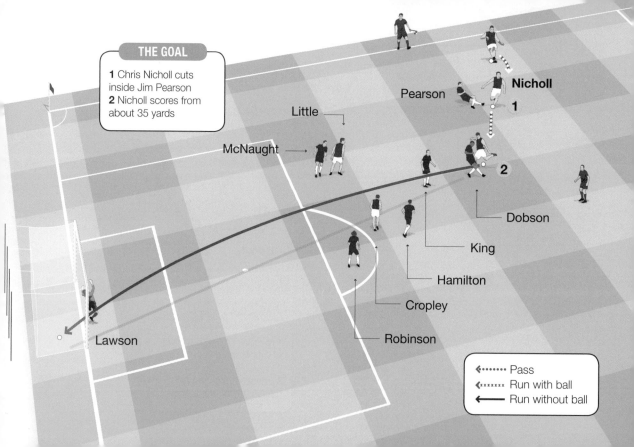

THE GOAL

1 Chris Nicholl cuts inside Jim Pearson
2 Nicholl scores from about 35 yards

Nicholl
1

Pearson

Little

McNaught

2

Dobson

King

Hamilton

Cropley

Robinson

Lawson

◀┄┄┄┄ Pass
◀┄┄┄┄ Run with ball
◀━━━━ Run without ball

021 CHRIS NICHOLL
Aston Villa v Everton, 13 April 1977
The screamer from the back

A year earlier Chris Nicholl had spawned a trivia question when he provided all four goals in a 2–2 draw when playing for Aston Villa away to Leicester City. Twice his own goals gave Leicester the lead and twice he netted at the right end to bring the scores level. Here there was a kind of mini-reprise. Having conceded the free-kick from which Everton took the lead, the central defender supplied the spectacular equaliser.

The match was a curiosity as the only second replay ever staged in the final of an English domestic competition or European club tournament. The first game ended 0–0 and after a 1–1 draw in the first replay it took a month before the teams could find time to play a third match.

Just as Manchester United have enjoyed many glorious cup games at Villa Park,

winning seven FA Cup semi-finals there, one of Villa's greatest cup nights came at United's Old Trafford ground.

But they were heading for disappointment before, with ten minutes remaining, Nicholl strode forward boldly from his centre back station and smashed the ball into the far corner of the goal.

Villa were halfway through a ten-year rise from third-tier side to European champions and this was a significant step on that journey. Even though Brian Little's winning goal for Villa came dramatically with only a minute of extra-time left, thus preventing a penalty shoot-out in a tie that lasted five and a half hours, the abiding memory of the game remains Nicholl's long-range strike.

"I did what I always did in that situation, and that was panic. I hit it as hard as I could" Chris Nicholl

---

THE MATCH

League Cup final second replay Old Trafford

Aston Villa 3
Nicholl 80, Little 81, Little 119
Everton 2
Latchford 38, Lyons 84
Att: 54,749

022 LIONEL MESSI
Barcelona v Panathinaikos, 14 September 2010
The lightning one-twos

One advantage of football over rugby as a spectator sport is that all aspects of the game are visible and not – as is the case with the oval-ball pursuit – sometimes obscured by a pile of bodies. Yet so quick are Lionel Messi's feet and mind that it can be almost impossible for onlookers to comprehend his actions fully as he skips past outwitted opponents in the blink of an eye.

That certainly applied here in a match when the Argentina forward scored twice for Barcelona and added two assists. Three days earlier he had played in an unthinkable 2–0 home defeat by little Hercules in the Spanish league but, after Panathinaikos had taken an early lead, he made sure there was no repeat.

This was the first fixture for Barcelona in a Champions League campaign that was to end in victory over Manchester United in the final. Given that they also lifted the trophy in 2009 and arguably deserved to do so in 2010, they were clearly Europe's dominant team, and their success was based on swift passing between short and nimble players. For this goal Messi was helped by Xavi and Pedro, all three of them no more than 5ft 7in tall.

Messi was the orchestrator, first exchanging passes with Xavi. Then, having moved into the D, he played an even tighter one-two with Pedro, a manoeuvre that occurred in a blur, and dispatched a low shot into the corner of the net. Messi could be forgiven for having his second-half penalty saved – he had done enough for one night.

"I played wall-passes with Xavi and then Pedro – it turned into a beautiful piece of play" Lionel Messi

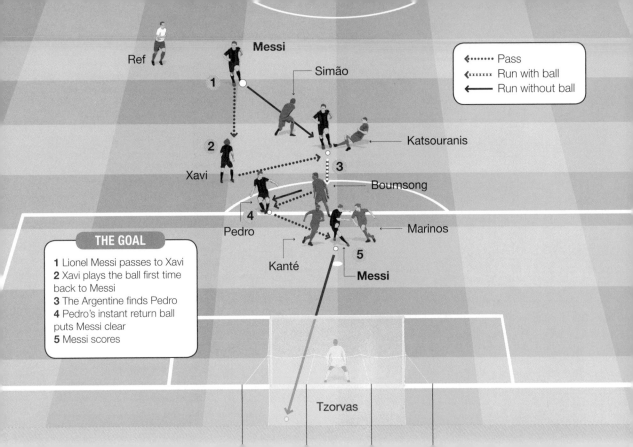

Ref

Messi

1

Simão

2

Xavi

Katsouranis

3

Boumsong

4

Pedro

Marinos

Kanté

5

Messi

←·······	Pass
←·······	Run with ball
←———	Run without ball

THE GOAL

1 Lionel Messi passes to Xavi
2 Xavi plays the ball first time
back to Messi
3 The Argentine finds Pedro
4 Pedro's instant return ball
puts Messi clear
5 Messi scores

Tzorvas

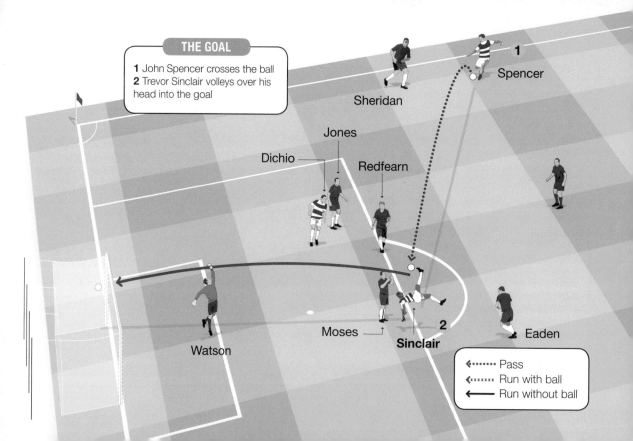

THE GOAL

1 John Spencer crosses the ball
2 Trevor Sinclair volleys over his head into the goal

Sheridan

Spencer

1

Jones

Dichio

Redfearn

Moses

Sinclair

2

Watson

Eaden

◀┄┄┄┄ Pass
◀┅┅┅┅ Run with ball
◀━━━━ Run without ball

023 TREVOR SINCLAIR
Queens Park Rangers v Barnsley, 25 January 1997
The gymnastic volley

Barnsley fans were fond of singing "It's just like watching Brazil" during the 1996–97 season, when the team played an attractive brand of football that secured promotion to the top flight for the first time. They might have said the same when Trevor Sinclair scored the goal that effectively brought an end to their club's FA Cup hopes in that same campaign.

Sinclair had shown great potential when he left Blackpool for Queens Park Rangers to play in the Premier League for the first time, impressing with his pace and trickery on the left-wing. He appeared for the England Under-21 team and was invited to train with the senior squad in 1995, but a year later his team were relegated, prompting months of speculation over whether he would return to the top flight by joining another club.

That prospect became more likely after this game. Sinclair was hardly a regular goalscorer – this was his only goal in his final 24 appearances of the season – but he knew exactly what to do when John Spencer's high cross fell to him on the edge of the penalty area. The winger delivered a bicycle kick that sent the ball over the head of goalkeeper David Watson and under the crossbar.

A year later he was back in the Premier League when he transferred to West Ham United, and eventually he wore an England shirt. Barnsley supporters would have understood that international call-up. When his volley found the net at Loftus Road, many of them applauded. In the tribalism of football, there is no greater accolade.

THE MATCH

**FA Cup fourth round
Loftus Road**

Queens Park Rangers 3
Peacock 20, Spencer 26, Sinclair 74
Barnsley 2
Redfearn 13, Hendrie 86
Att: 14,317

"I try them all the time in training but they've never come off like that"
Trevor Sinclair

024 BOBBY CHARLTON
England v Mexico, 16 July 1966
The gallop through the centre

Bobby Charlton's forty-nine goals for England remained a record four decades after his last appearance for his country yet he claimed his methods were simple. When given the chance to shoot, he would not aim for one particular part of the goal, but rather strike the ball as strongly as possible merely in the general direction of the net.

England fans had reason to be grateful for his expertise in this area of the game at the 1966 World Cup, where the team had failed to score in their first two hours of action despite playing on their own turf. "We want goals", was the chant from the stands, as Alf Ramsey's side followed their goalless draw with Uruguay with a turgid opening half-hour against Mexico.

The Mexicans packed their defence to great effect and were only breached when the breakdown of one of their rare forays forward allowed England to counter-attack quickly, catching them off guard. Ramsey's side were known as the Wingless Wonders and they lived up to their name on this occasion, taking a central route after Martin Peters had intercepted a pass and found Roger Hunt.

The ball was moved on to Charlton at the base of the centre circle and he set off, crossing the halfway line in a direct path before jinking to the right slightly to skirt round Gustavo Peña. He then let fly from 25 yards and the ball crashed into the far corner of the net. He had set England on their way, and two weeks later he and his team-mates would be holding the World Cup aloft.

"I just banged it and it came off so sweetly"
Bobby Charlton

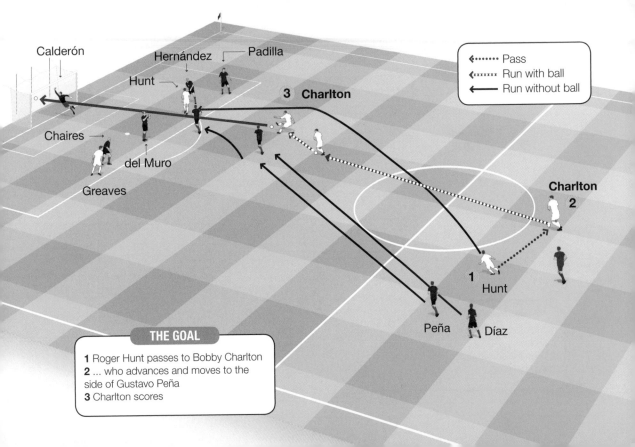

Calderón

Hernández — Padilla

Hunt →

3 Charlton

Chaires →

del Muro

Greaves

Charlton
2

Pass
Run with ball
Run without ball

1
Hunt

Peña Díaz

THE GOAL

1 Roger Hunt passes to Bobby Charlton
2 ... who advances and moves to the
side of Gustavo Peña
3 Charlton scores

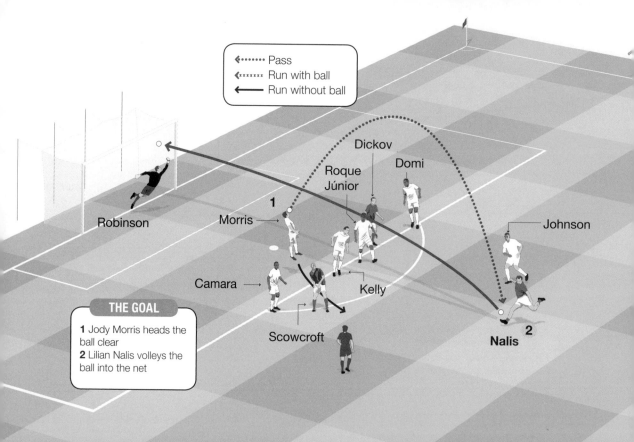

Pass
Run with ball
Run without ball

Robinson

Morris

1

Roque
Júnior

Dickov

Domi

Johnson

Camara

Kelly

THE GOAL

Scowcroft

Nalis

2

1 Jody Morris heads the ball clear
2 Lilian Nalis volleys the ball into the net

025 LILIAN NALIS

Leicester City v Leeds United, 15 September 2003
The twist and thump

A long-haired midfielder who wore Leicester City's No 8 shirt, Lilian Nalis was a reminder of Robbie Savage, who had spent five years at the club during their recent boom period. And on this night, at least, the Frenchman was able to match the popularity of his predecessor among the team's fans as he struck a spectacular volley with his weaker foot.

Nalis was no high-profile foreign star. A free transfer signing for Leicester from Chievo, his six years in England came in his thirties, and only the first of those was in the Premier League. In that season his 22 appearances produced just one goal, but he could reflect on it fondly.

Leeds United were suffering for their overspending during their Champions League days, which had forced the sale of several leading players. Their disarray was summed up by the fact that Roque Júnior was picked for this match despite having had only one training session with the club. He was among five on-loan players and also one of two debutant defenders, and he struggled in Leeds' biggest away league defeat for seven seasons.

Not that he could have foiled Nalis, who smashed a left-footed volley from 30 yards past Paul Robinson after pouncing on a headed clearance by Jody Morris. It was the opening goal in a 4–0 rout but Nalis, nicknamed Tarzan, could not stop the newly promoted Leicester swinging straight back down again as they managed only six wins all season. Leeds kept them company on their journey to relegation.

THE MATCH

**English league
Walkers Stadium**

Leicester City 4
Nalis 20, Dickov 23,
Dickov 83, Scowcroft 90
Leeds United 0
Att: 30,460

"It was my best goal ever and it meant a lot to me because it was my first for Leicester" Lilian Nalis

026 JOHN BARNES
Brazil v England, 10 June 1984
The diagonal dart

Having missed qualification for the 1984 European championship, which was starting two days later, England needed a pick-me-up.

It was provided by a win away to the biggest name in international football at the iconic Maracanã, the largest stadium in the world at the time. As if that were not enough, they took the lead with a classic goal by a youngster who had not previously scored for his country.

England manager Bobby Robson made what was considered a brave decision to field an inexperienced side, but perhaps he had nothing to lose. Eight days earlier the Wembley crowd had booed off his team after a dismal 2–0 home defeat by the USSR, and England had not beaten Brazil in their previous 11 attempts, which, at the time, was their longest barren run against any opponent in their history. Oh, and the Brazilians had not lost at the Maracanã for 27 years.

Mark Hateley, the Portsmouth striker who, later in the match, would mark his first England start by scoring the second goal, began the move for the opening goal by winning the ball and sending it to Barnes on the left. The 20-year-old Watford winger then set off on the run for which he will be forever remembered.

Cutting inside on a diagonal path, he accelerated to beat Leandro, changed direction to evade Ricardo Gomes, wrong-footed Pires and took the ball round goalkeeper Roberto Costa before sliding it home. It was a goal, supposedly, that only Brazilians were capable of scoring.

"The Brazilians were in shock. They thought there's no way an Englishman is going to do this" John Barnes

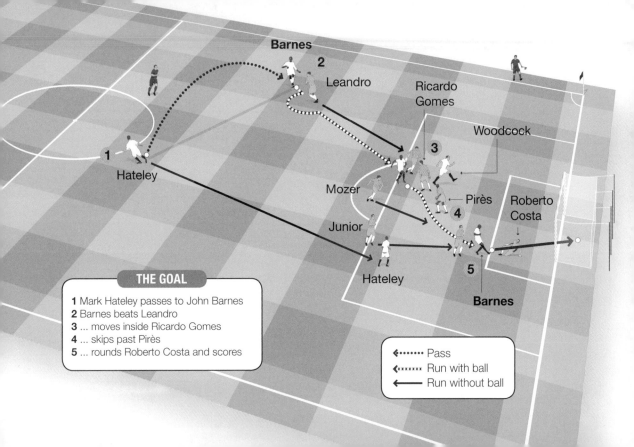

Barnes

2

Leandro

Ricardo Gomes

Woodcock

3

Hateley

1

Mozer

Pirès

4

Roberto Costa

Junior

Hateley

5

Barnes

THE GOAL

1 Mark Hateley passes to John Barnes
2 Barnes beats Leandro
3 ... moves inside Ricardo Gomes
4 ... skips past Pirès
5 ... rounds Roberto Costa and scores

◄········ Pass
◄┉┉┉┉ Run with ball
◄─── Run without ball

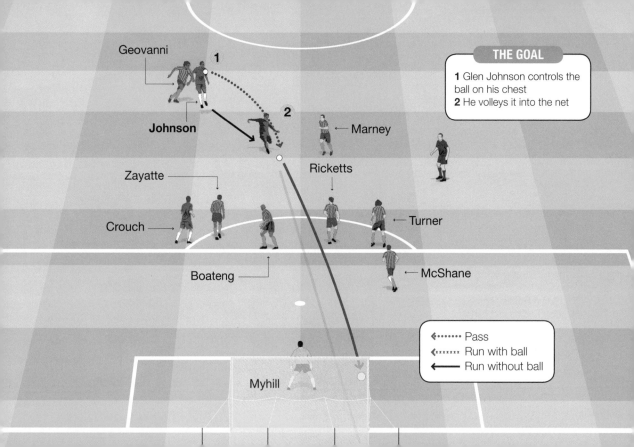

Geovanni

1

Johnson

2

Marney

Ricketts

Zayatte

Crouch

Turner

Boateng

McShane

Myhill

Pass
Run with ball
Run without ball

027 GLEN JOHNSON
Portsmouth v Hull City, 22 November 2008
The wrong-footed rifle

Glen Johnson holds the distinction of having been, in 2003, the first player signed by Chelsea during the Roman Abramovich era, but four years later he was part of another spending spree. Portsmouth were a smaller club than Chelsea but they acquired sufficient high-class talent to lift the FA Cup in 2008 and finish in the Premier League's top ten twice in a row.

However, whereas Chelsea could rely upon their Russian owner to continue to fund wages or pay bills, Portsmouth ran out of money. In the 15 months after they won the FA Cup they were forced to sell Johnson, Lassana Diarra, Jermain Defoe, and Peter Crouch for a combined £62 million in 2010. Despite that income they entered administration and were relegated.

They were still living beyond their means when Hull City visited Fratton Park in November 2008. Just three days earlier four Portsmouth players – Johnson, Defoe, Crouch and David James – had helped England win a friendly away to Germany, and on this occasion Crouch headed them in front against Hull. But Johnson, who scored just four times in 100 appearances for the club, produced a far more memorable goal.

When a Portsmouth cross was headed clear, the right-footed Johnson sprang forward from his right-back position, controlled the ball on his chest and, from around 30 yards out, volleyed it with his left foot into the far corner of the net. It was yet another high point for Portsmouth fans, but the club's great days were coming to an end.

"I had a couple of strikes with my left foot before I scored. Maybe I ought to start doing it a bit more often" Glen Johnson

---

THE MATCH

**English league
Fratton Park**

Portsmouth 2
Crouch 20, **Johnson 63**
Hull City 2
Turner 54, Windass 89
Att: 20,240

028 HENRIK LARSSON
Sweden v Bulgaria, 14 June 2004
The flying header

The clamour in Sweden for Henrik Larsson to end his international retirement and play at Euro 2004 was intense. A newspaper petition three months before the tournament in Portugal was signed by 110,000 people while UEFA president Lennart Johansson, a Swede, wrote a letter to the player pleading the case.

At first Larsson was adamant there would be no U-turn, but eventually he relented and proceeded to show why the Swedish public were so keen for his return. The striker inspired his side to reach the quarter-finals, where they only lost in a penalty shoot-out after a goalless draw with Holland. His three goals in the group stage included a spectacular header against Bulgaria.

That year Larsson had become the Scottish Premier League's leading scorer for a fourth season in a row. But if some observers felt his goals for Celtic lacked value because they came mostly against weak opposition, the player showed at Euro 2004 that he could also thrive at the highest level. In the 5–0 win over Bulgaria in Lisbon he set up the fifth goal by Marcus Allbäck, started and finished the move for the third and, most memorably, scored the second.

Erik Edman, the Sweden full-back, advanced down the left and struck a deep, curling cross just in front of Larsson as the forward hared into the penalty area. Larsson took off, hurling himself full length to ensure his head connected perfectly with the ball, which crashed into the corner of the net. All those signatures had borne fruit.

THE MATCH

European championship group game
Estádio José Alvalade

Sweden 5
Ljungberg 32,
Larsson 57, Larsson 58,
Ibrahimovic pen. 78,
Allbäck 90+1
Bulgaria 0
Att: 31,652

"It is easy to be a coach if you have someone like Larsson"
Sweden coach Lars Lagerbäck

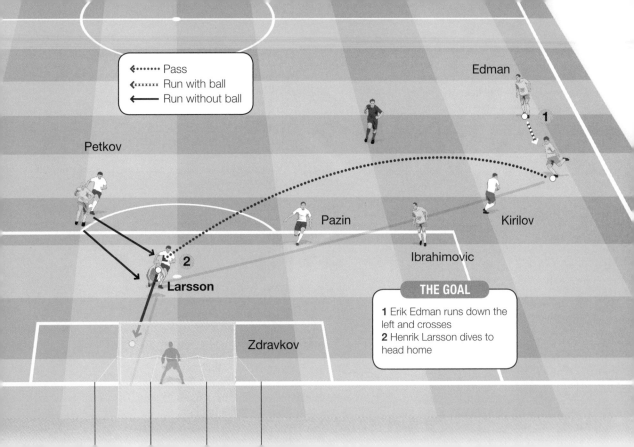

Pass

Run with ball

Run without ball

Edman

Petkov

1

Pazin

Kirilov

Ibrahimovic

2

Larsson

Zdravkov

THE GOAL

1 Erik Edman runs down the left and crosses

2 Henrik Larsson dives to head home

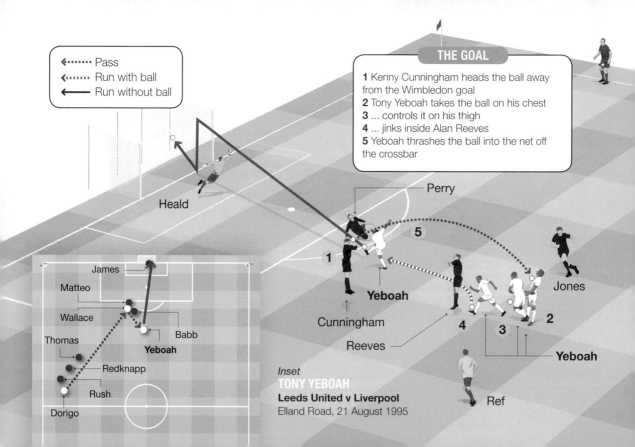

Pass ⬅······

Run with ball ⬅······

Run without ball ⬅──

THE GOAL

1 Kenny Cunningham heads the ball away from the Wimbledon goal
2 Tony Yeboah takes the ball on his chest
3 ... controls it on his thigh
4 ... jinks inside Alan Reeves
5 Yeboah thrashes the ball into the net off the crossbar

Heald

Perry

5

1

Yeboah

Jones

Cunningham

4

3

2

Reeves

Yeboah

Ref

Inset
TONY YEBOAH
Leeds United v Liverpool
Elland Road, 21 August 1995

James

Matteo

Wallace

Babb

Thomas

Yeboah

Redknapp

Rush

Dorigo

029 TONY YEBOAH

Wimbledon v Leeds United, 23 September 1995
The rising rocket

Tony Yeboah was born on 6-6-66, and early in the 1995–96 season the Leeds United striker lived up to his date of birth, knocking Liverpool and Wimbledon for six with spectacular long-range strikes that were remarkably similar.

Both shots were delivered with such force that the ball cannoned down off the underside of the crossbar and shot up again into the roof of the net. Furthermore, both efforts were hit from a central area just outside the penalty box and found the net on the right-hand side of the goal. The ball had moved like lightning, and lightning had struck twice.

Yeboah was among a new wave of African players in the English game, three of whom pitched up at Elland Road. Lucas Radebe and Phil Masinga, the South Africans, signed in the summer of 1994 and in the New Year they were joined by Yeboah, the Ghanaian striker, who arrived from Eintracht Frankfurt. He made his mark straight away, with his first nine starts bringing him nine goals, including a hat-trick against Ipswich Town.

But he made an even greater imprint on English football's consciousness at the start of the next season with his astonishing goals at Elland Road and Selhurst Park. The first was a volley, while the second, which was part of a hat-trick, was hit on the half-volley after he had controlled the ball smartly and cut inside Alan Reeves. Liverpool and Wimbledon were both defeated as Leeds, thanks to Yeboah, picked up the points – six of them in total, naturally.

"Once I get a sight of goal, I just love to have a go. I enjoy scoring spectacular goals" Tony Yeboah

---

THE MATCH

**English league
Selhurst Park**

Wimbledon 2
Holdsworth 43,
Reeves 58
Leeds United 4
Palmer 32, Yeboah 42,
Yeboah 45, Yeboah 73
Att: 13,307

030 CRISTIANO RONALDO
Manchester United v Portsmouth,
30 January 2008 The dipping free-kick

If the defensive wall is positioned properly, a free kick taker should face two options: power or direction. He could strike the ball hard and low, hoping it finds the net by squeezing through a tiny gap or taking a deflection; or he could hit the ball so that it flies over the wall but is moving slowly enough to drop under the crossbar.

Unless his name is Cristiano Ronaldo, in which case he can achieve power and direction at the same time. When the Portuguese demonstrated that ability for Manchester United against Portsmouth, it felt as though new possibilities were opening up. If a player is capable of doing this at every free kick, the goalkeeper is removed from the equation – the shot is unsaveable.

Opponents in general were finding Ronaldo impossible to stop. This was his 25th goal in 20 games and in the coming months he would retain both his FWA and PFA player of the year awards. At the end of the following season Real Madrid would pay United £80 million for him, £50m more than any English club had received for a player.

Real doubtless recalled this free kick when they offered that fortune. Ronaldo, with body over the ball, struck it with a straight boot, clearing the wall and producing a dramatic dip that left David James, the Portsmouth goalkeeper, helpless on his 500th top-flight appearance. United, who would lift the Premier League and Champions League trophies a few months later, struck 25 shots that night, but few were talking about the other 24 afterwards.

"The power made it impossible to save"
Joe Jordan, Portsmouth coach

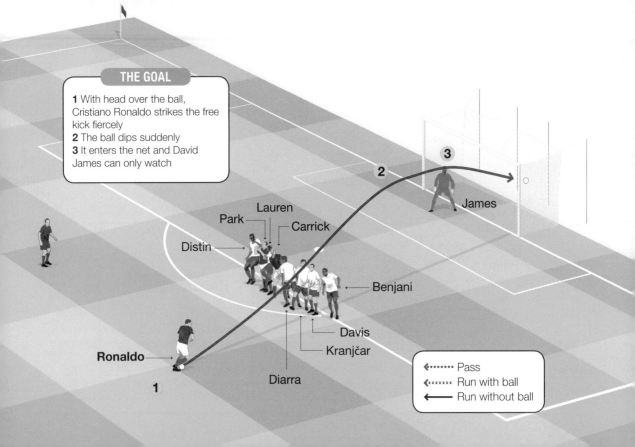

THE GOAL

1 With head over the ball, Cristiano Ronaldo strikes the free kick fiercely
2 The ball dips suddenly
3 It enters the net and David James can only watch

James

Lauren
Park
Carrick
Distin

Benjani

Davis
Kranjčar

Ronaldo

Diarra

1

2

3

←······· Pass
←······· Run with ball
←——— Run without ball

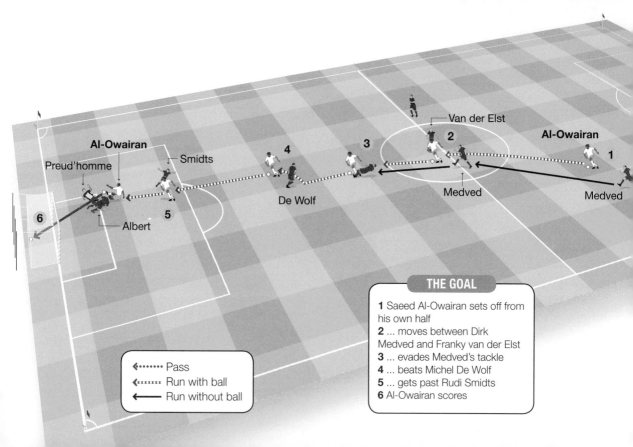

Van der Elst

Al-Owairan

Preud'homme

Al-Owairan

Smidts

1

4

3

2

De Wolf

Medved

Medved

5

6

Albert

THE GOAL

1 Saeed Al-Owairan sets off from his own half

2 ... moves between Dirk Medved and Franky van der Elst

3 ... evades Medved's tackle

4 ... beats Michel De Wolf

5 ... gets past Rudi Smidts

6 Al-Owairan scores

◄┄┄┄┄ Pass
◄┄┄┄┄ Run with ball
◄──── Run without ball

031 SAEED AL-OWAIRAN
Saudi Arabia v Belgium, 29 June 1994
The loping run

Temperatures were nudging 40 degrees centigrade at lunchtime in Washington, decidedly more Riyadh than Brussels. Yet Belgium could not blame the heat for Saeed Al-Owairan's solo goal for Saudi Arabia, since tiredness could hardly have set in only five minutes into the game.

Furthermore, even though the Saudis were playing in their first World Cup, the Belgians should not have been surprised by Al-Owairan's barnstorming run. He had been moved from attack to midfield in recent months specifically to help the team's counter-attacks, and he was known for his strength and energy. All those features were evident in his epic run to goal.

Saudi Arabia had lost narrowly to Holland and beaten Morocco, so victory here seemed possible. That was underlined when Al-Owairan gathered the ball in his own half after a Belgian attack. He ran between Dirk Medved and Franky Van der Elst, evaded Michel De Wolf, stumbled past Rudi Smidts and lifted his shot over goalkeeper Michel Preud'homme and Philippe Albert.

Having inspired his team to become the first from Asia to progress beyond the group stage at a World Cup, Al-Owairan was feted on his return home. But some time later he was caught drinking during Ramadan in Saudi Arabia and received a prison sentence and a one-year suspension from football. He claimed the penalty was stiff only because he was a celebrity in his country. While the rest of the world could enjoy his goal, Al-Owairan grew to have mixed feelings.

"It was the best goal I ever scored. I scored it for every Saudi person in the world, for every Arab" Saeed Al-Owairan

032 SHAUN BARTLETT
Charlton Athletic v Leicester City, 1 April 2001
The volley from the sky

Charlton Athletic became strongly associated with South Africa when ten players from that country joined the club in the first ten years after World War Two. One of those, Eddie Firmani, even went on to manage the club. That link was revived half a century later when their team featured Mark Fish and, to Leicester City's disappointment on this day, Shaun Bartlett.

Fish and Bartlett were helping Charlton to become the new Leicester – a middle-sized club punching above their weight in the Premier League, far from relegation danger. This was the second of eight consecutive league defeats for a Leicester side starting to decline after their success under the management of Martin O'Neill, who had left the previous summer. Charlton, newly promoted, were establishing themselves with Alan Curbishley at the helm.

This result was significant in the two clubs' paths as it took Charlton above Leicester, and Bartlett was heavily involved. The striker was not a prolific goalscorer but his aerial ability gave him value as a target man. This was emphasised when he headed the ball against the crossbar and Andy Todd scored the opening goal from the rebound.

Charlton's second goal, however, demonstrated how Bartlett could also be effective if he let the ball fall a little further out of the sky. When Graham Stuart's long, diagonal pass found him on the left side of the penalty area, he volleyed it first-time into the far corner. Still on loan from FC Zurich at this stage, he was, not surprisingly, signed permanently soon afterwards.

THE MATCH

English league
The Valley

Charlton Athletic 2
Todd 33, Bartlett 82
Leicester City 0
Att: 20,043

"It's something where it either goes ten feet over or straight into the corner" **Charlton manager Alan Curbishley**

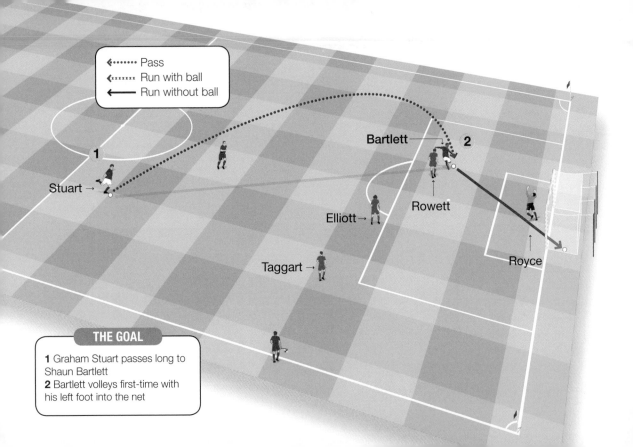

Pass
Run with ball
Run without ball

1

Stuart →

Bartlett

2

Rowett

Elliott →

Taggart →

Royce

THE GOAL

1 Graham Stuart passes long to Shaun Bartlett
2 Bartlett volleys first-time with his left foot into the net

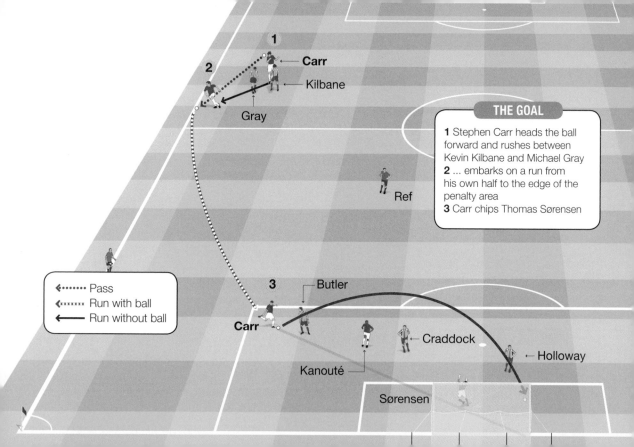

1

2

← **Carr**

← Kilbane

Gray

Ref

THE GOAL

1 Stephen Carr heads the ball forward and rushes between Kevin Kilbane and Michael Gray
2 ... embarks on a run from his own half to the edge of the penalty area
3 Carr chips Thomas Sørensen

◀······· Pass
◀······· Run with ball
◀——— Run without ball

3 ┌ Butler

Carr

Kanouté ─┘

← Craddock

← Holloway

Sørensen

033 STEPHEN CARR
Tottenham Hotspur v Sunderland, 14 May 2000
The charge and chip

After six months of searching, Stephen Carr finally gave up and retired. His contract at Newcastle United had not been renewed and, at 32, it seemed no other club wanted him. But two months later, in February 2009, he got his boots out again when Birmingham City came calling. He would play in two more Premier League campaigns and collect a League Cup winners' medal in 2011.

If it took a long time for any club to realise Carr's worth in his thirties, his contributions were fully recognised a decade earlier by Tottenham Hotspur fans, who voted him player of the year twice in a row when the likes of Darren Anderton, Sol Campbell and David Ginola were also at the club. His reliability at right back was his main attribute, but he did weigh in with a couple of remarkable goals in that period.

Carr was a rare scorer – he had only managed eight when he passed 400 league appearances – but Manchester United could not forget how, in October 1999, he advanced from his full-back position to shoot into the top-left corner. On the last day of that season against Sunderland he did even better, beating Kevin Kilbane and Michael Gray in his own half, dashing to the edge of the penalty area and executing a brilliantly controlled chip.

Even Tottenham's bigger-name players had to step back to allow Carr his rare moment in the full glare of the spotlight.

THE MATCH

English league
White Hart Lane

Tottenham Hotspur 3
Anderton pen 11,
Sherwood 73, Carr 83
Sunderland 1
Makin 20
Att: 36,070

"I remember just running down the wing and there wasn't really a lot on for me. I saw the keeper off the line, so had a go at chipping him" Stephen Carr

034 ASHLEY COLE
Chelsea v Sunderland, 16 January 2010
The control and clip

Roman Abramovich's lavish spending on new players helped end Chelsea's 50-year wait to become English champions in 2005, but soon their Russian owner was demanding more razzmatazz for his roubles. José Mourinho had achieved two consecutive league titles as manager without stirring his master's imagination, while Avram Grant and Luiz Felipe Scolari, his successors, had removed some of the team's caution without winning trophies.

In 2009 Carlo Ancelotti was charged with finding the magic formula and he was a spectacular success in his first season. This victory over Sunderland constituted the first time Chelsea had scored more than six goals in a top-division game for 49 years. To prove it was no fluke, they performed the feat another three times before the end

of a season in which they won the Premier League and the FA Cup.

During Mourinho's reign Ashley Cole barely crossed the halfway line, but the left-back was encouraged to attack by Ancelotti. By half-time against Sunderland, when he was substituted with an injured ankle, Cole had set up a goal for Frank Lampard and scored with one of three attempts himself.

That goal was a gem. Fellow defender John Terry struck an inch-perfect, lofted pass for Cole to control brilliantly on the left edge of the penalty area. When Sunderland's Lorik Cana lunged at the ball Cole simply dragged it back, waited for his opponent to slide off the pitch and flicked a shot over the goalkeeper, Márton Fülöp. No doubt Abramovich nodded approvingly.

"I would like to see Chelsea play every game like this. It is my dream" Chelsea manager Carlo Ancelotti

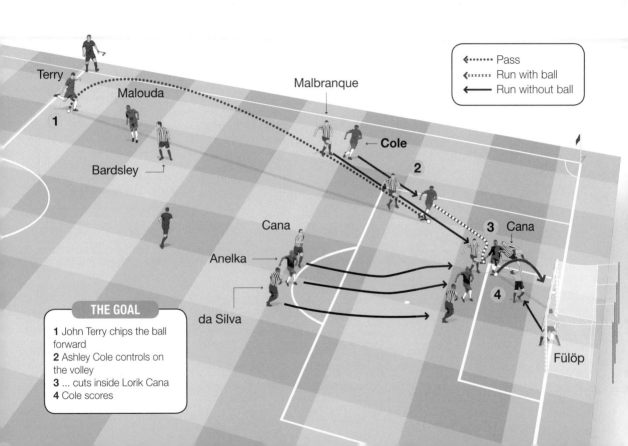

Terry

Malouda

Bardsley

Malbranque

Cole

2

Cana

Cana

3

Anelka

da Silva

4

Fülöp

◄······· Pass
◄········ Run with ball
◄─────── Run without ball

THE GOAL

1 John Terry chips the ball
forward
2 Ashley Cole controls on
the volley
3 ... cuts inside Lorik Cana
4 Cole scores

1

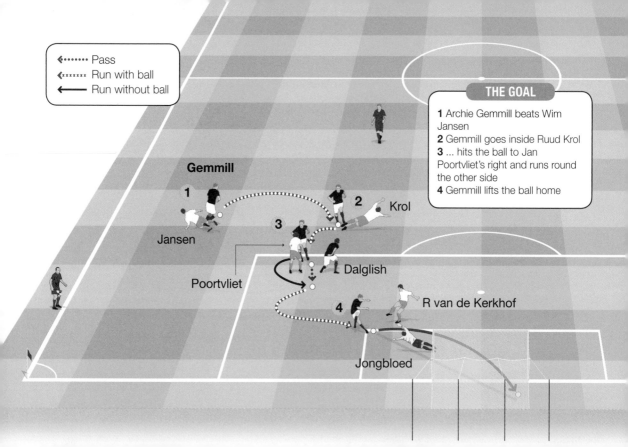

Pass
Run with ball
Run without ball

THE GOAL

1 Archie Gemmill beats Wim Jansen
2 Gemmill goes inside Ruud Krol
3 ... hits the ball to Jan Poortvliet's right and runs round the other side
4 Gemmill lifts the ball home

Gemmill

Krol

Jansen

Poortvliet

Dalglish

R van de Kerkhof

Jongbloed

035 ARCHIE GEMMILL
Scotland v Holland, 11 June 1978
The jink and dink

Having just helped Nottingham Forest become English champions in their first season after promotion – a feat unmatched since then – Archie Gemmill was accustomed to success against the odds. After Scotland lost to Peru and drew with Iran in their dismal opening matches at the 1978 World Cup in Argentina, he was again placed in the position of underdog for what proved to be the defining game of his career.

To reach the next round Scotland needed a three-goal victory in Mendoza against a fine Holland side that would finish the tournament – as they had done at the previous World Cup – as runners-up. The demoralised Scots were given little chance, especially when they fell behind just past the half-hour mark.

Even so, there were signs that the Dutch were worried about Gemmill's ability. Johan Neeskens, one of their leading players, was substituted after injuring himself when he lunged at the little Scottish midfielder. Scotland scored either side of half-time to move ahead and then came perhaps the nation's most memorable footballing moment.

Gathering possession near the right touchline, Gemmill left Wim Jansen and Ruud Krol on the ground as he skipped past them, knocked the ball one side of Jan Poortvliet, ran round the other side to collect it, and then clipped a shot past Jan Jongbloed. Scotland's realistic hopes of progressing to the next round survived for the three minutes that elapsed until Holland replied with a second goal, but Gemmill's goal will live forever in the memory.

"It's very pleasurable that people are still talking about it"
Archie Gemmill

036 THIERRY HENRY
Arsenal v Manchester United, 1 October 2000
The spinning spectacular

Fabien Barthez returned for this match after injury but the Manchester United goalkeeper might as well have stayed in the treatment room for all he could do about Thierry Henry's stunning volley. His knowledge of Henry's game – the pair were team-mates three months earlier when France won Euro 2000 – was of little use when the striker flashed an instant shot into the net well beyond his reach.

The goal came out of the blue in both timing and manner. England's best two teams had produced a tedious opening half-hour before Henry struck, and there seemed no immediate danger for United when the Frenchman received the ball with his back to goal on the edge of the penalty area. But he flicked it up to his left to escape Denis Irwin, his marker, and a split-second later his shot was heading for the top corner and Arsenal were heading for a victory.

The goal underlined how Henry was establishing himself in the Premier League after a slow start following his signing from Juventus. In the previous autumn he scored only once in his first 13 games for the club but now, fully settled in his new habitat, he was able to oversee a first defeat in 22 league games for United.

Henry also scored Arsenal's only goal in the league game away to United five months later, but United's six goals in reply that day confirmed that he would have to wait before earning the first English league winners' medal – it would come in 2002 – that his talents richly deserved.

THE MATCH

**English league
Highbury**

Arsenal 1
Henry 30
Manchester United 0
Att: 38,146

"The goal took your breath away. It was so spectacular. He'll never do that again" **Manchester United manager Sir Alex Ferguson**

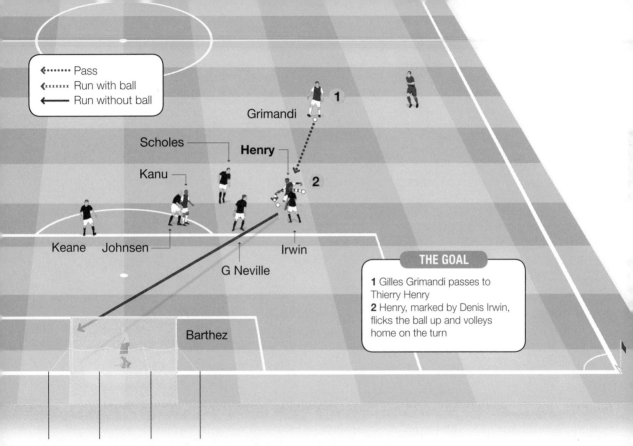

Pass
Run with ball
Run without ball

Grimandi

1

Scholes

Henry

Kanu

2

Keane   Johnsen

Irwin

G Neville

THE GOAL

1 Gilles Grimandi passes to Thierry Henry
2 Henry, marked by Denis Irwin, flicks the ball up and volleys home on the turn

Barthez

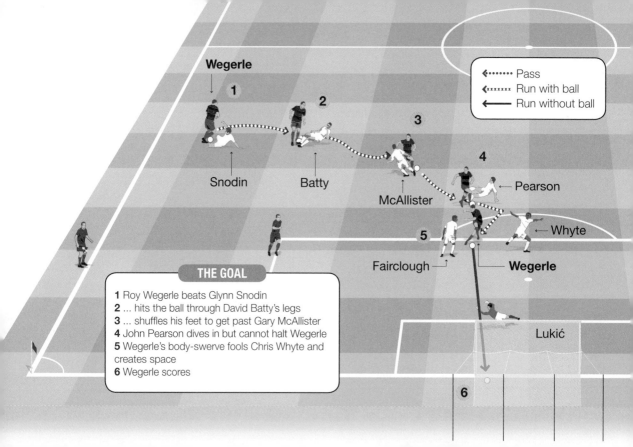

Wegerle

1

2

3

4

Pearson

Snodin

Batty

McAllister

Whyte

5

Fairclough →

Wegerle

- ┄┄┄ Pass
- ┈┈┈ Run with ball
- ──── Run without ball

THE GOAL

1 Roy Wegerle beats Glynn Snodin
2 ... hits the ball through David Batty's legs
3 ... shuffles his feet to get past Gary McAllister
4 John Pearson dives in but cannot halt Wegerle
5 Wegerle's body-swerve fools Chris Whyte and creates space
6 Wegerle scores

Lukić

6

037 ROY WEGERLE
Leeds United v Queens Park Rangers,
20 October 1990 The six-step sizzler

**English league
Elland Road**

Leeds United 2
Whyte 15, Chapman 17
Queens Park Rangers 3
Wilkins 29, **Wegerle 40**,
Wegerle 80
Att: 27,443

Roy Wegerle was a United States international footballer who was born in South Africa to a Scottish mother and German father and was now playing in England. If readers are confused by a quick reading of that sentence then their feelings are matched by the bewilderment felt by half the Leeds United team who faced the Queens Park Rangers player at Elland Road in 1990.

As Wegerle wove his way through the defence, it was a reminder of the kind of flair shown by Rodney Marsh, a predecessor of his in the QPR No10 shirt. Perhaps Marsh had passed on some ideas. After all, he was Wegerle's first manager when the youngster joined Tampa Bay Rowdies, the American club, straight from college.

Collecting the ball on the right-hand flank, Wegerle jumped over Glynn Snodin's sliding tackle, waited for David Batty to leap into a challenge before slipping the ball through his legs, beat Gary McAllister with a stepover, accelerated and prodded the ball forward to evade the diving John Pearson, jinked to wrong-foot Chris Whyte and drove a low shot just inside the post.

Wegerle, who later completed QPR's comeback from 2–0 down with the winning goal, could eventually gain extra satisfaction from his amazing dribble by considering the fact that few opponents got the better of Leeds over the next two years. After this defeat the Yorkshire club won their subsequent eight home league matches to finish fourth in the table. A year later they were champions.

"It was probably the best goal I ever scored"
Roy Wegerle

038 RIVALDO
Barcelona v Valencia, 17 June 2001
The overhead kick

Romario, Ronaldo, Rivaldo, Ronaldinho: Barcelona welcomed these four similar-sounding Brazilian forwards between 1993 and 2008. They never overlapped at the Nou Camp, instead making their mark alone. Rivaldo's main imprint on the club's history undoubtedly came in this game.

Barcelona had won only four of their previous 16 league fixtures when they hosted Valencia in their last game needing a win to secure the fourth and final Champions League place ahead of their opponents. Rivaldo had already shown he could handle the big occasion: that season he had scored a hat-trick away to AC Milan and was only denied a treble away to Real Madrid by a close offside call.

Here, already into the second half of June, the Brazilian again showed he could take the heat. Three times he scored from outside the penalty area against Santiago Cañizares, the first-choice Spanish international goalkeeper, curling a free kick over the wall and in off a post for the first goal and beating Kily González before sending a shot skidding into the net for the second.

During an impoverished childhood Rivaldo's walk to training was a 15-mile round trip and his endurance helped Barcelona here. In the last minute of the season he still had the energy to control Frank de Boer's chipped pass forward, teeing himself up with a chest flick and curling a fierce overhead kick inches inside the post. At that moment, the Nou Camp would have believed Rivaldo could walk 15 miles on water.

"Rivaldo does not need the team to play well around him. He can win games on his own" **Barcelona coach Carles Rexach**

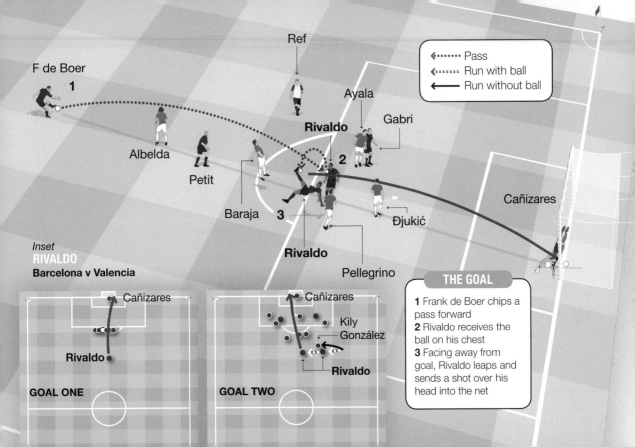

F de Boer

1

Pass
Run with ball
Run without ball

Ref

Ayala

Rivaldo

Gabri

Albelda

Petit

2

Baraja

3

Đjukić

Cañizares

Inset
RIVALDO
Barcelona v Valencia

Rivaldo

Pellegrino

Cañizares

THE GOAL

Cañizares

Kily
González

1 Frank de Boer chips a
pass forward
2 Rivaldo receives the
ball on his chest
3 Facing away from
goal, Rivaldo leaps and
sends a shot over his
head into the net

Rivaldo

Rivaldo

GOAL ONE

GOAL TWO

039 MARCO VAN BASTEN
Holland v USSR, 25 June 1988
The impossible angle

Given subsequent events it was remarkable that Marco van Basten was considered good enough only for the substitutes' bench when Holland opened their 1988 European championship campaign with a 1–0 defeat by USSR. By the time he led his side to victory over the same opponents in the final, he was being hailed as one of the world's finest players.

Van Basten scored a hat-trick as England were beaten 3–1 in Holland's second game, and expertly slid home the late winning goal against West Germany, the hosts, in the semi-final. But those feats were merely the appetiser for the striker's incredible goal in the final.

Arnold Mühren's cross rose so high that van Basten, waiting close to the byline on the right edge of the penalty area, had time to ponder his options. Instead of trying to control the ball – a tricky enough task – he chose to attempt a first-time volley, and it flew into the only part of the net not covered by Rinat Dasayev, the great Soviet goalkeeper.

Rinus Michels had guided a much-admired Holland team to the 1974 World Cup final, where they lost to West Germany, and here he was back in the same stadium in Munich striving again to give his country their first major trophy. Van Basten's astounding goal prompted him to put his hand over his head in a mixture of bewilderment and delight. Michels had fallen short with Johan Cruyff and co in 1974, but van Basten had helped him achieve his dream 14 years later.

"I have to be thankful that such a moment was given to me"
Marco van Basten

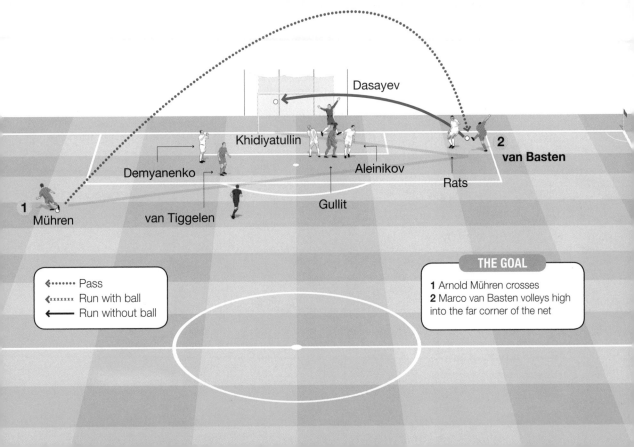

Dasayev

Khidiyatullin

Demyanenko

Aleinikov

2
van Basten

Rats

Gullit

van Tiggelen

1
Mühren

········ Pass
········ Run with ball
─────── Run without ball

THE GOAL

1 Arnold Mühren crosses
2 Marco van Basten volleys high
into the far corner of the net

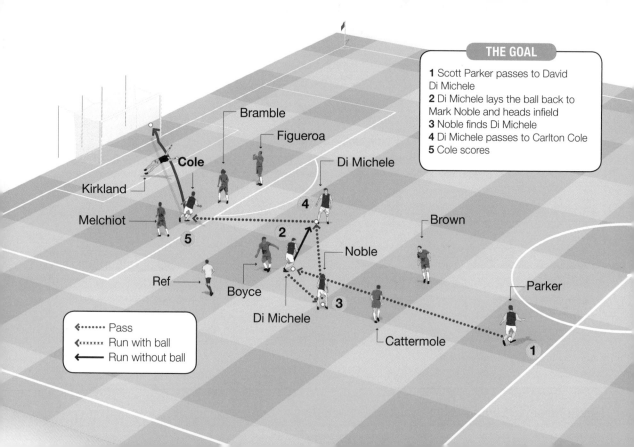

Bramble

Figueroa

Di Michele

Cole

Kirkland

Melchiot

4

Brown

5

2

Noble

Ref

Boyce

Di Michele

3

Parker

1

Cattermole

THE GOAL

1 Scott Parker passes to David Di Michele
2 Di Michele lays the ball back to Mark Noble and heads infield
3 Noble finds Di Michele
4 Di Michele passes to Carlton Cole
5 Cole scores

- - - - - Pass
- - - - - Run with ball
——— Run without ball

040 CARLTON COLE
Wigan Athletic v West Ham United, 4 March 2009
The five-touch fantasy

For ten minutes West Ham United went wild. Mark Noble was booked for tripping Lee Cattermole, then Carlton Cole and Scott Parker saw yellow for fouls on Michael Brown and, finally, Cole was sent off for a second bookable offence when his boot caught Emmerson Boyce in the face – after which Parker had to be restrained as he remonstrated with Brown for demanding Cole's dismissal.

Yet somehow, in the middle of that short, ugly burst, there was still time for Noble, Parker and Cole to contribute to a goal of stunning beauty. If the whole episode was reminiscent of Jekyll and Hyde, then so was the career of Cole, the striker who finished off that memorable one-touch move.

A powerful player with great potential, he had been on Chelsea's books from the age

of 17 but made only four league starts for them in five years as he was sent away for three loan spells. After joining West Ham he won seven England caps yet was turning out for the club in the second tier while still in his twenties.

But here West Ham were in the Premier League, where their manager, the former Chelsea star Gianfranco Zola, was enhancing their reputation for sophisticated play. This was evident in Cole's goal, for which the last five touches were each delivered first-time – four passes and the shot. Parker found David Di Michele, who exchanged passes with Noble while drifting infield. The Italian then sent Cole through to curl the ball home. Minutes later, after his dismissal, Cole could reflect on the goal at his leisure.

"The creation and the build-up were magnificent, and it was great finishing" Gianfranco Zola, West Ham manager

041 ANDRÉS D'ALESSANDRO
Charlton Athletic v Portsmouth, 17 April 2006
The conjuring trick in the corner

Harry Redknapp had returned for his second spell as Portsmouth manager a month earlier and was up to his old tricks. A shrewd operator in the transfer market, he took full advantage of the January window, acquiring nine senior players as he battled to overcome the poor start to the season made by his predecessor, Alain Perrin, and steer the team away from the relegation zone.

The last of the nine players to arrive at the club was the most remarkable. Andrés D'Alessandro's left-footed wizardry had drawn praise from Diego Maradona, his Argentine compatriot, and he had already won more than 20 caps at the age of 24 when he agreed to move to the ramshackle Fratton Park ground on loan from German club Wolfsburg.

D'Alessandro had escaped Redknapp's grasp in the past when, as West Ham United manager, he rejected the creative midfielder after a trial because he was too similar in style to Joe Cole, who was already at the club. The Argentine showed what Redknapp had missed by helping Portsmouth mount a successful and highly unlikely charge to safety, although his greatest moment came in a defeat against Charlton Athletic.

Collecting the ball from a throw-in near the right-hand corner flag, D'Alessandro performed a series of drag-backs, foot shuffles and jinks to wriggle away from Chris Powell and Radostin Kishishev and curl the ball into the top corner of the net. He would leave Portsmouth for Spain in the summer, his mission for Redknapp accomplished.

THE MATCH

English league
The Valley

Charlton Athletic 2
Hughes 76, D Bent 83
Portsmouth 1
D'Alessandro 40
Att: 25,419

"What a superb goal – he is a man who can make things happen"
TV commentator Jonathan Pearce

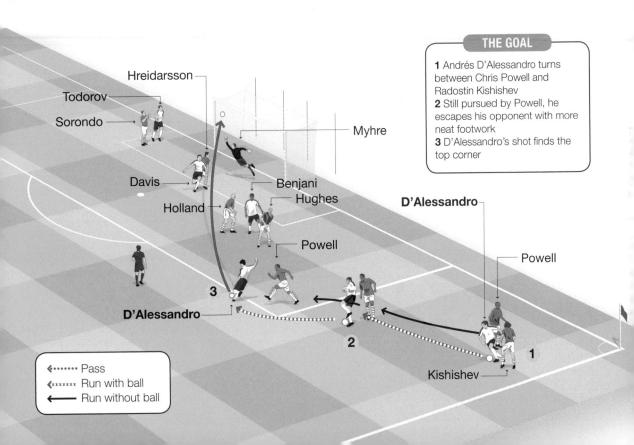

Hreidarsson

Todorov

Sorondo

Myhre

Davis

Holland

Benjani

Hughes

Powell

D'Alessandro

Powell

3

D'Alessandro

2

D'Alessandro

Kishishev

1

THE GOAL

1 Andrés D'Alessandro turns between Chris Powell and Radostin Kishishev
2 Still pursued by Powell, he escapes his opponent with more neat footwork
3 D'Alessandro's shot finds the top corner

••••••• Pass
:::::::: Run with ball
⟵⟵⟵ Run without ball

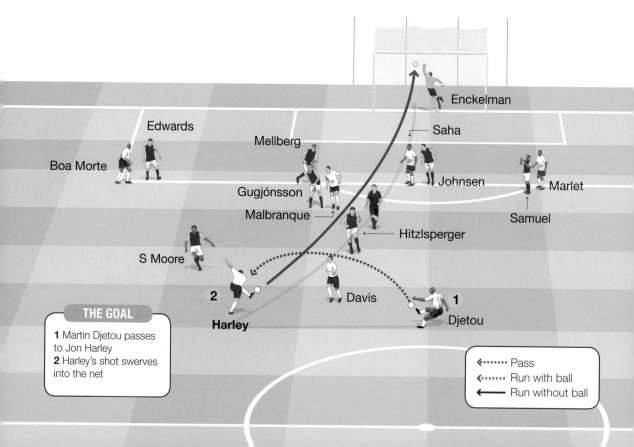

Enckelman

Edwards

Mellberg

Boa Morte

Gugjónsson

Malbranque

Hitzlsperger

Saha

Johnsen

Marlet

Samuel

S Moore

2

Harley

Davis

1

Djetou

THE GOAL

1 Martin Djetou passes to Jon Harley

2 Harley's shot swerves into the net

◄······· Pass
◄:::::::: Run with ball
◄——— Run without ball

042 JON HARLEY
Fulham v Aston Villa, 8 February 2003
The bolt from the blue

Jon Harley spent more than two years at Fulham but it took just one second of spectacular action to transform him from what would have been a largely forgotten figure among the club's fans to one now recalled with some fondness. Martin Djetou knocked a pass sideways and Harley, running onto the ball 35 yards out, did not think twice as he sent what seemed an outrageously optimistic shot flying in an arc past goalkeeper Peter Enckelman.

If the goal itself was unlikely, so was the scorer: Harley, a left back, averaged about one league goal per season. His strengths, rather, were tidy passing and accurate crossing, which had been impressive enough to earn him a Chelsea debut at 18 and consideration for an England squad place at Euro 2000 when just 20.

But he did not establish himself at Stamford Bridge and an international call would never come. Fulham sent him out for three brief loan spells and his subsequent clubs were Sheffield United, Burnley, Watford and Notts County, all outside the Premier League when he was playing for them.

Aston Villa came into this match having won their previous two games by three-goal margins and they looked on course to continue that sequence when Gareth Barry gave them an early lead against Fulham. Then Steed Malbranque equalised with a penalty to start the turnaround. Steve Marlet and Louis Saha both missed from a couple of yards for Fulham, but Harley had no such trouble from much farther out.

"An incredible goal"
Peter Brackley, TV commentator

043 MAURO BRESSAN
Fiorentina v Barcelona, 2 November 1999
The distant bicycle kick

THE MATCH

**Champions League
group game
Stadio Artemio Franchi**

Fiorentina 3
Bressan 14, Balbo 56,
Balbo 69
Barcelona 3
Figo 20, Rivaldo 43,
Rivaldo 74
Att: 28,000

Italian clubs playing in the Champions League have been packed with star names over the years but Mauro Bressan was not among them. A midfielder who never appeared for Italy, he was a journeyman who moved club 12 times in his career. When he spent two years at Fiorentina, the strongest of those teams, he struggled to establish himself as a first-choice player.

In the 1999–2000 season Bressan started only six Italian league games for Fiorentina, making far more appearances as a substitute, and he also started just two of their 14 matches in the Champions League. He was hardly a regular goalscorer either, managing only two goals in the league in his time at the club and one in European competition – but what an incredible goal that was.

If his spell at Fiorentina represented the peak of his career, then his spectacular bicycle kick against Barcelona was the greatest moment by far. Perhaps he was encouraged by the sense of adventure when these clubs met. They shared 12 goals in their two Champions League group games, the Spanish side winning 4–2 at home and this return match ending 3–3.

As the ball bounced high several yards outside the penalty area, with a crowd of players between him and the goal, Bressan seized the moment. Leaping two feet off the ground, he was horizontal when he hooked a shot that flew in an arc over Francesc Arnau. The people of Florence had another work of art to enjoy.

"Oh my word, that's stunning"
TV commentator Peter Drury

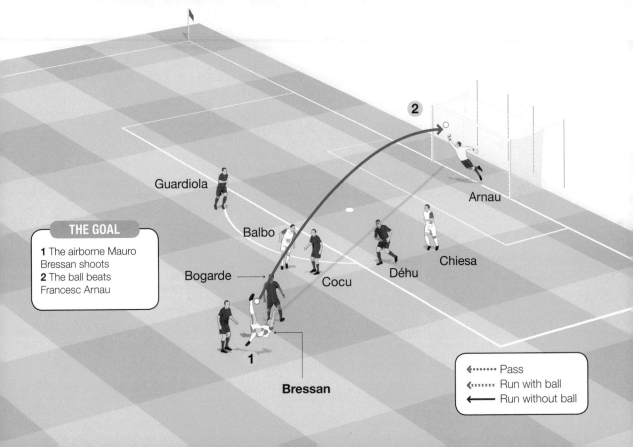

THE GOAL

1 The airborne Mauro Bressan shoots
2 The ball beats Francesc Arnau

Guardiola

Balbo

Bogarde →

Cocu

Déhu

Chiesa

Arnau

2

1

Bressan

◄······· Pass
◄······· Run with ball
◄─── Run without ball

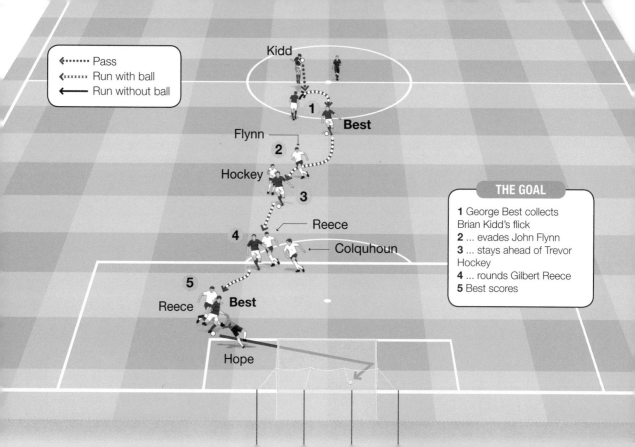

Kidd

------- Pass
------- Run with ball
—— Run without ball

1

Best

Flynn

2

Hockey

3

Reece

4

Colquhoun

5

Reece **Best**

Hope

THE GOAL

1 George Best collects
Brian Kidd's flick
2 ... evades John Flynn
3 ... stays ahead of Trevor
Hockey
4 ... rounds Gilbert Reece
5 Best scores

044 GEORGE BEST
Manchester United v Sheffield United, 2 October 1971 The roundabout route

The so-called "refs' revolution" at the start of the 1971–72 season was aimed at protecting entertainers such as George Best. Any cynical foul was to bring an automatic yellow card, and the conclusion among observers was that football became more watchable as a result. It might even have contributed to one of the great goals.

Sheffield United arrived at Old Trafford as unexpected league leaders following their promotion, and with their manager, Tony Waddington, describing his squad as having been "picked up in Woolworth's rather than Harrods". One player fitting this description was Trevor Hockey, a rugged midfielder whose job was to repel more skilful opponents. His image was reinforced by his beard – the only one in the top division at the time (although Best himself wore one at other stages of his career).

Hockey was among three Sheffield United players who were close enough to have been capable of impeding Best (as opposed to actually winning possession) as the Irishman sped with the ball from near the centre circle to deep inside the penalty area, always heading slightly to the right. But, perhaps mindful of the disciplinary clampdown, they let him go, and the Manchester United forward topped off his wandering run by angling his shot inside the far post.

Until that point, six minutes from time, the match had been goalless and evenly contested. But Best's intervention ended the visitors' unbeaten record and left him joint top of the league goalscorers' chart. He was certainly a Harrods player.

"Only George could have scored that one"
Manchester United manager Frank O'Farrell

THE MATCH

**English league
Old Trafford**

Manchester United 2
Best 84, Gowling 86
Sheffield United 0
Att: 51,735

045 JULIANO BELLETTI
Wigan Athletic v Chelsea, 3 November 2007
The rush down the right

Juliano Belletti scored Barcelona's late winner against Arsenal in the 2006 Champions League final and his handful of goals for Chelsea also tended towards the dramatic. This strike against Wigan Athletic was his first for the London side, while two of his other four for the club were hit from around 30 yards out.

In the later stages of his Chelsea career Belletti often played in midfield but against Wigan he was a right-back, and his remarkable run began from this position. The Brazilian evaded a lunge by Jason Koumas as he played a one-two with Shaun Wright-Phillips, skipped past Denny Landzaat near the halfway line and advanced to the edge of the penalty area, from where he curled a shot around Titus Bramble, the defender, into the net.

If the goal was spectacular then the circumstances were routine. It meant Chelsea had already built a 2–0 lead after less than 20 minutes of the game as Wigan headed for a sixth defeat in a row while their opponents moved towards a seventh successive victory to continue their impressive recovery from the managerial departure two months earlier of José Mourinho, who had guided the club to their first two league titles in 50 years.

Belletti himself never quite became a first-choice during his three years at Chelsea but, as with his goals, his appearances were relatively scarce yet often memorable. His final two games for the club, in May 2010, were the 8–0 win over Wigan that clinched the league title and the FA Cup final victory against Portsmouth that completed the club's first double.

THE MATCH

English league
JJB Stadium

Wigan Athletic 0
Chelsea 2
Lampard 11, Belletti 18
Att: 19,011

"Quite magical"
Guy Mowbray, TV commentator

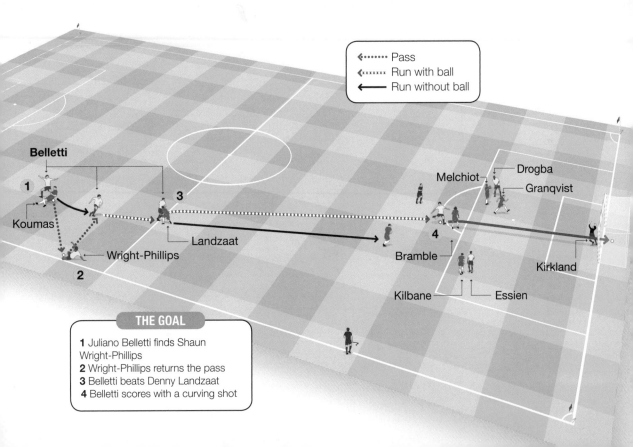

Pass
Run with ball
Run without ball

Belletti

1

Koumas

2

Wright-Phillips

Landzaat

3

Melchiot

Drogba

Granqvist

4

Bramble

Kirkland

Kilbane

Essien

THE GOAL

1 Juliano Belletti finds Shaun
Wright-Phillips
2 Wright-Phillips returns the pass
3 Belletti beats Denny Landzaat
4 Belletti scores with a curving shot

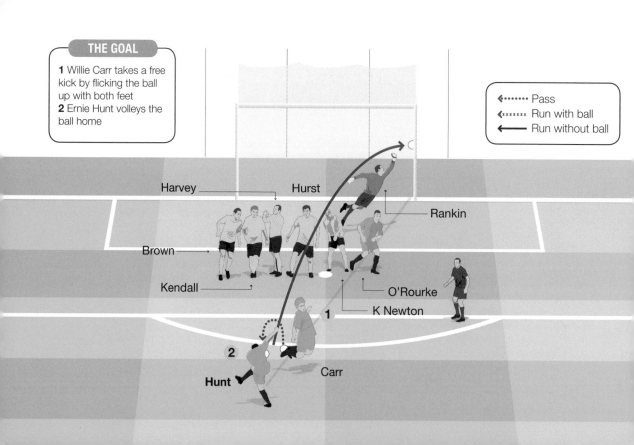

THE GOAL

1 Willie Carr takes a free kick by flicking the ball up with both feet
2 Ernie Hunt volleys the ball home

Pass
Run with ball
Run without ball

Harvey
Hurst
Rankin
Brown
Kendall
O'Rourke
K Newton
1
2
Hunt
Carr

046 ERNIE HUNT
Coventry City v Everton, 3 October 1970
The donkey kick

Coventry City fans were already in party mood when Everton, the champions, visited Highfield Road. On the previous day the Midlands club had been drawn to face Bayern Munich in the Fairs Cup in what was their first European campaign. What happened ten minutes from the end of this game only added to the carnival atmosphere.

Coventry had ended a run of four league games without scoring when they traded first-half goals with their opponents. But Ernie Hunt put them ahead on the hour and the forward made sure of victory when he finished off a free-kick routine that his team had been practising in training.

Hunt loitered as his team-mate, Willie Carr, stood with the stationary ball trapped between his feet just outside the D. What happened next was so unexpected that television was still showing the Everton wall when the free-kick was delivered to Hunt. A replay revealed that Carr had flicked the ball into the air with both feet. As it fell, Hunt stepped forward and smashed a shot on the volley over the wall and into the far corner of the net.

Later that season, when Coventry tried the same ruse, Hunt hit the Tottenham Hotspur crossbar. That summer, though, the manoeuvre was banned because the ball was considered not to have met the requirement of moving its full circumference before a second player touched it. At the time Hunt's goal against Everton was hailed as unique – that subsequent decision by world governing body FIFA meant it would stay so.

"It was a real circus trick, almost a whodunit"
Geoffrey Green, *Times* Football Correspondent

047 GARETH BALE
Inter Milan v Tottenham Hotspur, 20 October 2010
The acceleration and accuracy

THE MATCH

Champions League group stage
San Siro

Inter Milan 4
Zanetti 2, Eto'o pen. 11, Stankovic 14, Eto'o 35
Tottenham Hotspur 3
Bale 52, Bale 90, Bale 90+1
Att: 70,520

This defeat for Tottenham Hotspur felt like a victory; Gareth Bale trudged off the San Siro pitch beaten but utterly triumphant.

The English team recovered from crushing half-time deficits – four goals and one man down – to lose only 4–3, giving them the confidence not only to beat the Italian side 3–1 in the return Champions League group game, but also to inflict defeat on AC Milan back at the San Siro in the knock-out stage en route to the quarter-finals.

The previous nine months had transformed Bale from habitual unused substitute at White Hart Lane into one of the Premier League's best players. It was only here, though, that he came to global attention with a daring, destructive hat-trick, turning some of the world's greatest defenders to jelly.

Tottenham's lack of numbers after the early dismissal of goalkeeper Heurelho Gomes meant Bale had no team-mate ahead of him when, shortly after the break, he gathered the ball in his own half. Not that he needed one. The Welsh left-winger motored away from four South American luminaries – Brazilians Maicon and Lúcio; Argentines Javier Zanetti and Walter Samuel – and fired home.

The game entered the 90th minute still at 4–1 yet finished 4–3, courtesy of Bale. The fact that his three goals came from almost identical shots – low, left-footed drives across goal just inside the right-hand post – only added to the surreality. His feat confirmed him as a rarity: a non-Englishman who might win a place in a United Kingdom team.

"A year ago he [Bale] was nowhere near that player we see now"
Tottenham manager Harry Redknapp

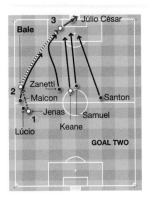

GOAL TWO

Júlio César
Bale — 3
2
Zanetti
Maicon
Jenas
Lúcio — 1
Santon
Samuel
Keane

GOAL THREE

3 — Júlio César
Lúcio
2
Bale — Samuel
Zanetti — 1
Lennon — Santon

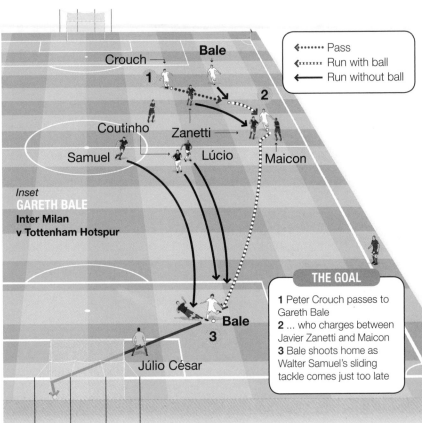

········• Pass
········ Run with ball
———→ Run without ball

Crouch →
Bale
1
2
Coutinho
Zanetti →
Samuel
Lúcio
Maicon

Inset
GARETH BALE
Inter Milan v Tottenham Hotspur

Bale
3

Júlio César

THE GOAL

1 Peter Crouch passes to Gareth Bale
2 ... who charges between Javier Zanetti and Maicon
3 Bale shoots home as Walter Samuel's sliding tackle comes just too late

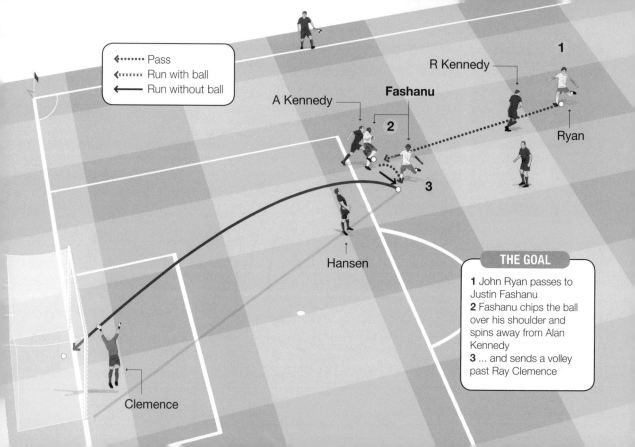

Pass
Run with ball
Run without ball

R Kennedy

1

Ryan

A Kennedy

Fashanu

2

3

Hansen

Clemence

THE GOAL

1 John Ryan passes to Justin Fashanu
2 Fashanu chips the ball over his shoulder and spins away from Alan Kennedy
3 ... and sends a volley past Ray Clemence

048 JUSTIN FASHANU
Norwich City v Liverpool, 9 February 1980
The Carrow Road arrow

There were eight goals: one voted the best of the season in English football, three of them equalisers in a seesaw match, and two scored very late by Liverpool as they grabbed victory. As the referee Mike Scott said after overseeing his first top-flight game: "After that I suppose you only go one way, and that's downhill." Sadly, Justin Fashanu could have said much the same.

Fashanu, just short of his nineteenth birthday, scored an extraordinary goal from long range for Norwich, and at 20 he would join Nottingham Forest for a £1million transfer fee, only two years after Trevor Francis had become English football's first £1m player. But he moved from club to club, struggling to fit in as he faced homophobia. At 37 he took his own life.

It was a tragic end, but on that day at Carrow Road he had the world at his feet after giving a scare to a Liverpool side about to retain their league title. They had been forced to change their line-up for the first time in 13 league games but David Fairclough, who replaced the injured David Johnson in attack, showed the squad's strength in depth by scoring a hat-trick to put his side 3–2 up.

Then came Fashanu's intervention. He flicked the ball away from Alan Kennedy and, from long range, volleyed home a swerving shot inches inside the far post. Liverpool then scored twice in the final three minutes but it could not deflect attention from Norwich's young striker.

THE MATCH

**English league
Carrow Road**

Norwich City 3
Peters 1, Reeves 33,
Fashanu 81
Liverpool 5
Fairclough 4, Fairclough 18, Fairclough 75, Dalglish 88, Case 89
Att: 25,624

"It was the best goal I've ever seen. You can't do anything about shots like that" **Liverpool defender Phil Thompson**

049 FRANK WORTHINGTON

Bolton Wanderers v Ipswich Town, 21 April 1979

The through ball … to himself

Frank Worthington played in eight successive matches for England in 1974 but otherwise his country ignored him, the fate of many gifted flair players of that era. He rarely scaled the heights in terms of club success either: only once, at Southampton in 1983–84, did he finish in the top six. Liverpool, a heavyweight side, did want him in 1972 but he failed a medical – his high blood pressure was attributed to his partying lifestyle.

Bolton Wanderers were only in the second tier when they signed Worthington in 1977 and, after promotion in his first season, they flirted with relegation in the next campaign. Not that the striker needed top-class team-mates to create all his shooting chances. When he scored in this game he also supplied the through pass.

After Worthington gathered a bouncing ball with his back to goal 15 yards out, he juggled it with his head and twice with his foot as Ipswich Town's defence followed him out of the penalty area. Then he flicked the ball over his shoulder, swivelled as he passed wrong-footed opponents and, now through on goal, volleyed home one of his 24 league goals that season, the most in the top flight.

Bolton were just another step on a long and varied journey taken by Worthington, who played for 11 league clubs and another dozen teams in the non-leagues or abroad. Just seven months after scoring this remarkable goal he dropped down a division to join Birmingham City, who became the next club to benefit from the player's restless and talented feet.

THE MATCH

English league
Burnden Park

Bolton Wanderers 2
Worthington 36,
Allardyce 74
Ipswich Town 3
Brazil 39, Wark 45,
Brazil 62
Att: 20,073

"A virtuoso mixture of skill, showmanship and breathtaking impudence" Peter Keeling, *Daily Telegraph*

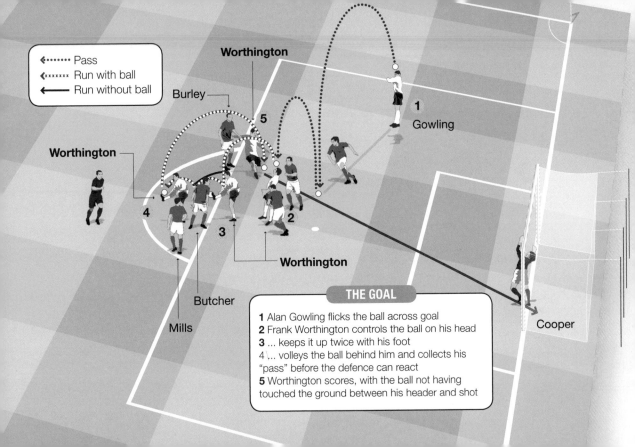

Pass
Run with ball
Run without ball

Worthington

Burley

Worthington

5

4

3

2

Butcher

Mills

Worthington

1

Gowling

Cooper

THE GOAL

1 Alan Gowling flicks the ball across goal
2 Frank Worthington controls the ball on his head
3 ... keeps it up twice with his foot
4 ... volleys the ball behind him and collects his "pass" before the defence can react
5 Worthington scores, with the ball not having touched the ground between his header and shot

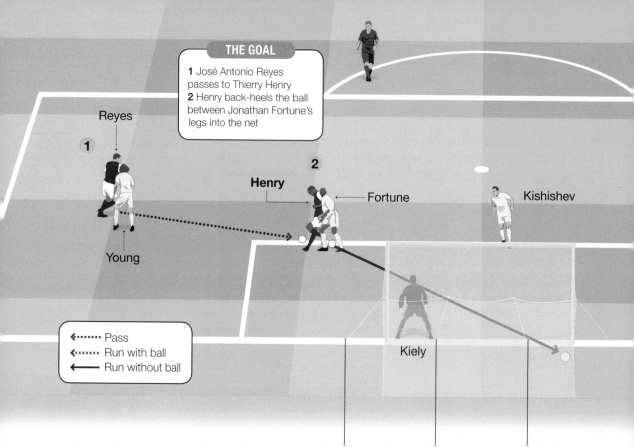

THE GOAL

1 José Antonio Reyes passes to Thierry Henry
2 Henry back-heels the ball between Jonathan Fortune's legs into the net

Reyes

1

2

Henry

Fortune

Kishishev

Young

Kiely

•••••• Pass
•••••• Run with ball
—— Run without ball

050 THIERRY HENRY
Arsenal v Charlton Athletic, 2 October 2004
The brilliant back-heel

A substitution seemed appropriate. Whatever Arsène Wenger's reasons for taking off Thierry Henry near the end of this game, the Arsenal manager's decision allowed the crowd to give the Frenchman a standing ovation, a proper recognition for the moment of genius that had illuminated their day.

The striker was familiar with acknowledgements of his talent. When he won both of English football's main player of the year awards in 2003 he might have expected to wait a while before collecting them again, given that no player had ever won either of them two years in succession. Yet he duly won both in 2004 as well, a few months before Charlton Athletic visited Highbury.

Arsenal, like Henry, were unstoppable at that moment. This was their 48th unbeaten league game in a row, six more than the previous record in English football. The sequence would come to a halt at 49, but on that afternoon at Highbury it felt as though it would never end, especially when Henry made his eye-catching intervention.

Charlton defender Jonathan Fortune was clinging to Henry's back in the penalty area. The striker, denied any space, surely had nowhere to go. One measure of an act of genius is that most players would not even have contemplated it. Henry simply back-heeled the ball through Fortune's legs and into the net. The Frenchman was the Premier League's top scorer in four out of five seasons from 2001 to 2006, but it was the style of his goals, rather than the bare figures, that live longer in the memory.

THE MATCH

**English league
Highbury**

Arsenal 4
Ljungberg 33,
Henry 48, Henry 69,
Reyes 70
Charlton Athletic 0
Att: 38,103

"It was fantastic. You don't see those goals very often. There's only one Thierry Henry" **England manager Sven-Göran Eriksson**

051 PETER CROUCH
Liverpool v Galatasaray, 27 September 2006
The acrobatic finish

For such a fine player Peter Crouch has endured a chequered career at club level. He only played his first top-flight match at 21 for Aston Villa – an advanced age for a future England forward – and then dropped a division at 22 to play on loan at Norwich City. Thereafter, often uncertain of his place in the team, he relocated so frequently that he had made his eighth permanent club move by the age of 30.

His longest spell at one club in that period was his three years at Liverpool, but that does not mean he established himself fully there. In fact Rafael Benítez, the manager, had left him out for the two matches before this one, warning him not to get carried away by his three goals in two England games earlier in the month.

Crouch, whose minutes-per-goal figure for England was better than all the greats, from Bobby Charlton and Jimmy Greaves to Gary Lineker and Michael Owen, was keen to prove a point against Galatasaray. He achieved that by meeting Steve Finnan's deep cross with an overhead kick that flew into the goal. Given that Benítez had warned him unnecessarily to keep his feet on the ground after his England heroics, scoring with a big leap seemed an apt response.

In contrast to the Champions League final 16 months earlier, when Liverpool won from 3–0 down against AC Milan in Galatasaray's Ataturk stadium in Istanbul, they nearly lost a three-goal lead here, holding on for a 3–2 win. So Crouch's scissor kick was decisive as well as a classic.

THE MATCH

Champions League group game
Anfield

Liverpool 3
Crouch 9, Luis García 14, Crouch 52

Galatasaray 2
Ümit 59, Ümit 65
Att: 41,976

"Most of the time they go over the stand when I try that"
Peter Crouch

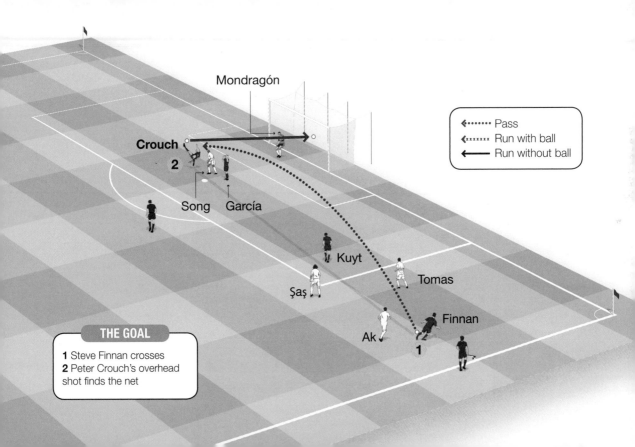

Mondragón

Crouch

2

Song   García

Kuyt

Tomas

Şaş

Ak   Finnan

1

◀······· Pass
◀┄┄┄┄ Run with ball
◀─── Run without ball

THE GOAL

1 Steve Finnan crosses
2 Peter Crouch's overhead
shot finds the net

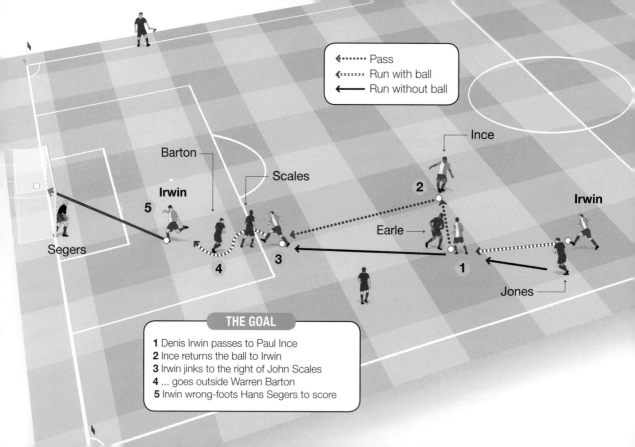

Pass
Run with ball
Run without ball

Ince

Barton

Scales

Irwin

5

2

Earle

Irwin

4

3

1

Segers

Jones

THE GOAL

1 Denis Irwin passes to Paul Ince
2 Ince returns the ball to Irwin
3 Irwin jinks to the right of John Scales
4 ... goes outside Warren Barton
5 Irwin wrong-foots Hans Segers to score

052 DENIS IRWIN
Wimbledon v Manchester United, 20 February 1994
The toying and the thrust

By finally ending their 26-year wait for the league title in the previous season Manchester United had removed the suffocating pressure to which they had become accustomed. Now they could simply concentrate on proving they had the best side in the country, a status that was undisputed as they headed towards a possible domestic treble.

It was a team in their prime. Only two of the XI that faced Wimbledon were under 25 yet none were over 30. Throw in the fact that the main players largely stayed free of injury that season and it was no great surprise that they were unbeaten in 31 games in all competitions before this FA Cup tie. To help them extend that run, 20,000 away fans filled most corners of Selhurst Park.

Denis Irwin was a fixture at left-back but had needed to work his way to the top. The Irishman was more interested in playing Gaelic football as a boy and had only appeared in the English second tier with Leeds United and Oldham Athletic before he moved to Old Trafford aged 24. His goal completed the scoring in what was perhaps United's strongest performance of the season.

United teased Wimbledon, holding the ball for 35 seconds, before Irwin added urgency, exchanging passes with Paul Ince, beating John Scales on one side and Warren Barton on the other and rolling his shot past Hans Segers. United lost the League Cup final to Aston Villa a month later but their first League and FA Cup double more than compensated for that.

"We looked just about invincible"
Manchester United manager Alex Ferguson

THE MATCH

**FA Cup fifth round
Selhurst Park**

**Wimbledon 0
Manchester United 3**
Cantona 42, Ince 63,
Irwin 71
Att: 27,511

053 MAYNOR FIGUEROA
Stoke City v Wigan Athletic, 12 December 2009
The 61-yard free kick

Perhaps Maynor Figueroa should thank referee Mike Dean for helping him make history. The Wigan Athletic defender will forever be renowned as the player who scored from a free-kick in his own half, yet the offence – Stoke City's Robert Huth fouled Scott Sinclair – occurred on the other side of the halfway line. The official was either unaware or unconcerned that the ball had rolled about six yards to the place where the Honduran took long-range aim.

Not that Figueroa was in the mood for hanging around to confirm the free-kick's correct location. As soon as the ball came to rest he darted forward and struck a fierce left-foot shot. This was not a vague aerial punt of a ball that eventually fell out of the sky and embarrassed a stumbling goalkeeper. Thomas Sørensen, in the Stoke goal, was only a couple of steps from his line when the ball was hit from 61 yards out, yet he was powerless to save it as the ball flew like an arrow just over his head and dipped into the goal.

Figueroa had seen his stock rise during Wigan's previous away game against Tottenham Hotspur even without playing. An injury meant the left back's defensive qualities were missed on a day when the opposition's right winger, Aaron Lennon, scored one goal and set up three more in a 9–1 victory. No wonder Roberto Martínez, the Wigan manager, said he would struggle to keep the Honduran after his free-kick showed he possessed some decent attacking qualities as well.

"You need to have a certain kind of arrogance even to try something like that" Wigan manager Roberto Martínez

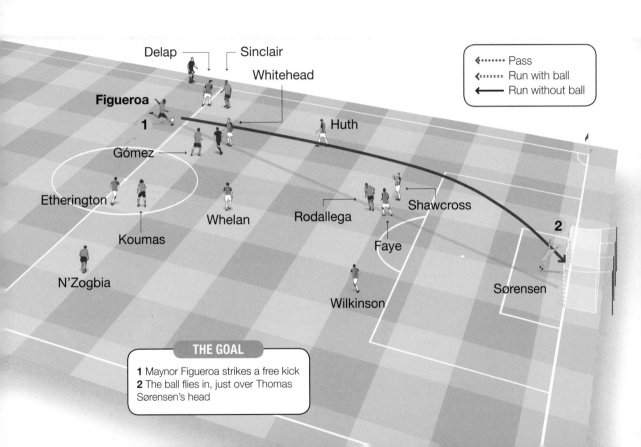

Delap — Sinclair

Whitehead

Figueroa

1

Gómez

Huth

Etherington

Koumas

Whelan

Rodallega

Shawcross

Faye

2

Wilkinson

Sørensen

N'Zogbia

◄······· Pass
◄····· Run with ball
◄───── Run without ball

THE GOAL

1 Maynor Figueroa strikes a free kick
2 The ball flies in, just over Thomas Sørensen's head

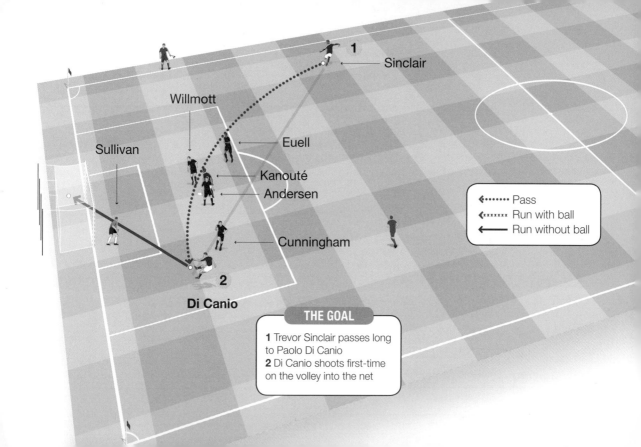

Sinclair

Willmott

Euell

Sullivan

Kanouté

Andersen

Cunningham

←······ Pass
←┄┄┄┄ Run with ball
←——— Run without ball

Di Canio

THE GOAL

1 Trevor Sinclair passes long to Paolo Di Canio
2 Di Canio shoots first-time on the volley into the net

054 PAOLO DI CANIO
West Ham United v Wimbledon, 26 March 2000
The scissors kick

Paolo Di Canio's genius had prompted Juventus and AC Milan to sign him in the past yet Harry Redknapp was widely considered to be taking a risk by bringing the Italian to West Ham United in January 1999. The concern was temperament rather than talent. Four months earlier, when playing for Sheffield Wednesday against Arsenal, he had responded to receiving a red card from Paul Alcock by pushing the referee to the ground.

That led to an 11-match suspension and a retreat to his native country, but Redknapp enticed him back to the Premier League. Over the years the manager has made a habit of reviving players whose careers have gone off the rails and his man-management skills helped coax the best out of Di Canio.

Perhaps the striker's greatest moment at West Ham came early in this match against Wimbledon when a diagonal pass by Trevor Sinclair found him on the left edge of the penalty area. Di Canio struck the ball instantly on the volley with the outside of his right foot, sending it flashing into the opposite corner of the net.

It was late March and Wimbledon's miraculous 14-year stay in the top division was almost over. After this defeat they took one point from their remaining eight league games and were relegated, three points from safety. The dream was over for their small band of followers, but West Ham supporters, grateful for Redknapp's initial act of faith in signing Di Canio, would enjoy three more years of watching the Italian in the Premier League.

"I was very lucky. I try that a lot in training but every time I miss"
Paolo Di Canio

055 MATT TAYLOR

Portsmouth v Everton, 9 December 2006
The low-flying missile

Matt Taylor has long been a far-sighted footballer. As a teenager playing for Luton Town against Cambridge United, he once took aim from 40 yards and sent the ball over the goalkeeper into the net. His talent for distant strikes was revealed to a broader public when he scored from a 40-yard half-volley for Portsmouth in the Premier League away to Sunderland in 2005, and he consolidated his ability by habitually practising long-range efforts in training.

But Taylor surpassed himself when he faced Everton at Fratton Park, a match he only played in after passing a test on his injured back before kick-off. With his fitness proved, he was in confident mood after scoring twice one week earlier to earn his side a 2–2 draw against Aston Villa.

Nearly a quarter of an hour had passed when Portsmouth striker Kanu challenged Simon Davies in the centre circle. The ball spun high into the path of Taylor, who, as if he had been expecting such an outcome, did not break stride before smashing home a volley.

Goalkeeper Tim Howard had not strayed far from his net yet he was powerless to act as the shot arrowed just over his head. It was also agonising for Everton's Alan Stubbs, a member of the Sunderland defence that had been beaten by Taylor's lengthy drive the previous season. Kanu struck an impressive second goal for Portsmouth, whose victory took them to the unimaginable heights of third place in the Premier League table, but the after-match talk centred on Taylor.

"You won't see a better strike than that for years"
Portsmouth manager Harry Redknapp

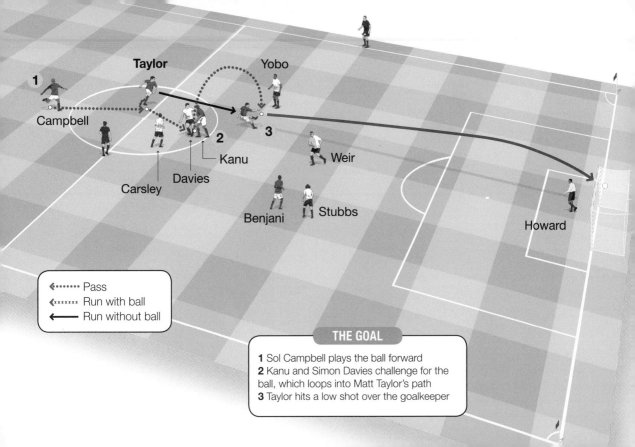

1

Taylor

Yobo

Campbell

Carsley

Davies

2

Kanu

3

Weir

Benjani

Stubbs

Howard

◄······· Pass
◄······· Run with ball
◄——— Run without ball

THE GOAL

1 Sol Campbell plays the ball forward
2 Kanu and Simon Davies challenge for the ball, which loops into Matt Taylor's path
3 Taylor hits a low shot over the goalkeeper

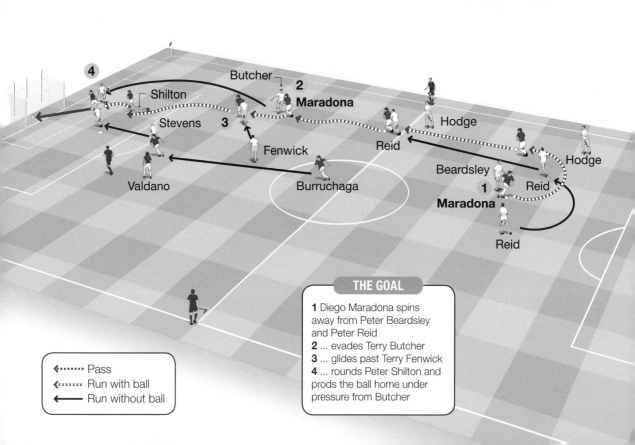

4

Butcher

2
Maradona

Shilton

Stevens

3

Fenwick

Hodge

Reid

Hodge

Beardsley

1

Reid

Maradona

Valdano

Burruchaga

Reid

THE GOAL

1 Diego Maradona spins
away from Peter Beardsley
and Peter Reid
2 ... evades Terry Butcher
3 ... glides past Terry Fenwick
4 ... rounds Peter Shilton and
prods the ball home under
pressure from Butcher

⬅······· Pass
⬅······· Run with ball
⬅——— Run without ball

056 DIEGO MARADONA
Argentina v England, 22 June 1986
The 60-yard wriggle

THE MATCH

**World Cup quarter-final
Aztec Stadium**

Argentina 2
Maradona 51,
Maradona 55
England 1
Lineker 81
Att: 114,580

Perhaps only Diego Maradona's unique blend of mischief and magic could produce two of football's most famous goals in the space of four minutes. The hand that was still red from punching the ball into England's net seemed to have waved a wand as he ran more than half the length of a heavy pitch in sweltering heat to double Argentina's lead.

Maradona dragged his country through their triumphant 1986 World Cup campaign in Mexico and there was no question of him edging out of the limelight in shame after his illegal goal. Instead he grabbed centre stage by taking on England himself.

With a 5ft 5in frame that was lowered further by his jinking, crouching style of dribbling, he almost tunnelled his way to a victory that was secured by his incredible goal. He wriggled away from Peter Beardsley and Peter Reid, crossed into England's half, body-swerved inside Terry Butcher and cut outside Terry Fenwick.

Maradona had now arrived in the penalty area but still he toyed with the English, with whom a national rivalry had developed, partly because of the Falklands War four years earlier. Out came Peter Shilton but Maradona moved right to pass the England goalkeeper and then held off a second challenge by Butcher to poke the ball into the net. All 12 of his touches during his incredible run were made with his left foot: why bother with the right when the left is so good? The build-up to the goal had featured three Peters and two Terrys but only one – there is only one – Diego.

"What planet have you come from to run through the English like that" **Victor Hugo Morales, commentator on Argentine TV**

057 PAUL GASCOIGNE
Tottenham Hotspur v Arsenal, 14 April 1991
The rising free kick

THE MATCH

**FA Cup semi-final
Wembley**

Tottenham Hotspur 3
Gascoigne 5,
Lineker 10, Lineker 78
Arsenal 1
Smith 45
Att: 77,893

Genius and craziness often co-exist and they could be found in Paul Gascoigne's contributions to Tottenham Hotspur's successful FA Cup campaign in 1990–91. Spurs only beat Nottingham Forest in the final after he departed early because of a self-inflicted injury sustained via his dreadful tackle on Gary Charles, but fans of the England midfielder prefer to remember his efforts in the previous round against Arsenal.

This was the first FA Cup semi-final between the North London neighbours and – partly as a result – the first held at nearby Wembley, which provided a fitting stage for Gascoigne's dramatic intervention.

He had only recently recovered from a hernia injury, which meant he lasted for just an hour before tiredness forced his substitution, but by then he had made his mark.

David Seaman, the Arsenal goalkeeper, would become known for conceding long-range goals in high-profile games, but, unlike Nayim's effort for Real Zaragoza in the 1995 Cup Winners' Cup final or Ronaldinho's free kick for Brazil against England in the World Cup quarter-finals in 2002, the goalkeeper could not be blamed on this occasion.

Five minutes had gone when Tottenham won a free kick 35 yards out and Gascoigne, who had inspired England's run to the World Cup semi-finals a year earlier, was confident enough to shoot. The ball was still rising as it struck the top right-hand corner of the net. In the battle between Gascoigne's two competing characteristics, it was, happily, genius that had won out on this occasion.

"It wasn't bad, was it?"
Paul Gascoigne

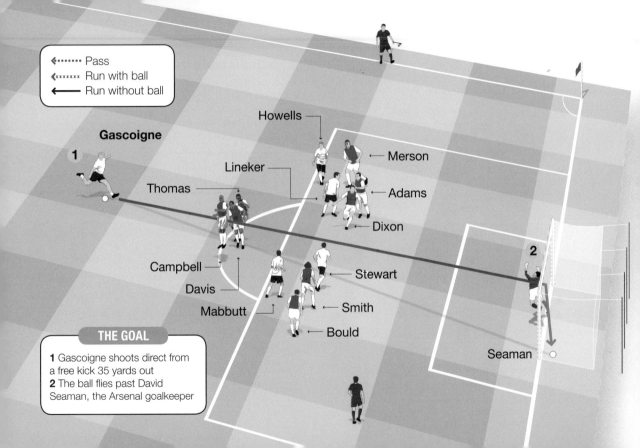

Pass
Run with ball
Run without ball

Gascoigne

1

Howells

Merson

Lineker

Thomas

Adams

Dixon

2

Campbell

Stewart

Davis

Mabbutt

Smith

Bould

Seaman

THE GOAL

1 Gascoigne shoots direct from a free kick 35 yards out
2 The ball flies past David Seaman, the Arsenal goalkeeper

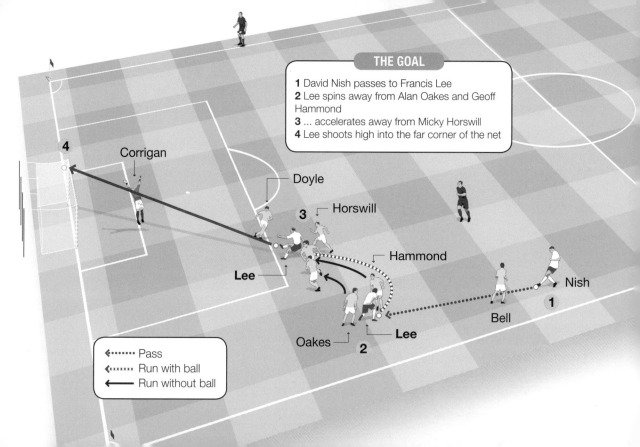

THE GOAL

1 David Nish passes to Francis Lee
2 Lee spins away from Alan Oakes and Geoff Hammond
3 ... accelerates away from Micky Horswill
4 Lee shoots high into the far corner of the net

4

Corrigan

Doyle

3 ⌐ Horswill

Hammond

Lee

Nish

1

Bell

Lee

Oakes

2

◄······· Pass
◄┄┄┄┄ Run with ball
◄━━━━ Run without ball

058 FRANCIS LEE
Manchester City v Derby County,
28 December 1974 The smash and smile

Francis Lee's legendary status at Manchester City was assured. He had helped them win the league in 1967–68, his first season at the club, collected three more winners' medals in different cup competitions over the next two years and, in 1973–74, completed five consecutive seasons as the team's leading (or joint-leading) goalscorer.

So Lee was hurt to discover in that summer of 1974 that City wanted to sell him even though he had only just turned 30. He moved to Derby County and ringed in his diary 28 December, the date when he would return to Maine Road with his new club and hope to prove a point. In the week before the match it was said he did not leave home other than to attend training, so keen was he to rest properly.

City began the game unbeaten at home in the league while Derby had only won twice away, but Lee was determined to overcome the odds. Playing alone in attack he harried opponents relentlessly, set up Derby's first goal and scored their second. For his goal, he wriggled away from Geoff Hammond, Alan Oakes and Micky Horswill as he cut in from the left and drove the ball into the top corner of the net. His grinning face as he ran away in celebration told the story.

Derby, stuck in mid-table at Christmas, held on to win the game and proceeded to climb the table quickly. When they – and their single-minded centre forward – were crowned league champions four months later, it was the final blow for City, the ultimate revenge for Lee.

"Look at his [Lee's] face. Just look at his face"
Barry Davies, TV commentator

THE MATCH

English league
Maine Road

Manchester City 1
Bell 64
Derby County 2
Newton 21, Lee 67
Att: 40,188

059 KAKÁ
AC Milan v Fenerbahçe, 13 September 2005
The silky saunter

The Champions League may have overtaken the World Cup as the pinnacle of football in the eyes of many observers but that doesn't mean Brazilians are excluded from the game at the highest level. In fact it is their exodus from South America to Europe that has helped create the all-powerful teams from Spain, Italy, England and Germany that have dominated the competition.

A total of 45 players from Brazil played in the first round of 16 Champions League group fixtures in 2005–06, among whom the leading figure was undoubtedly Kaká. Described as having the technique of a Brazilian and the physical qualities of a European by Wanderley Luxemburgo, the former Brazil coach, he stood tall at 6ft 1in yet was an outstanding dribbler.

This was Milan's first Champions League fixture since the previous season's final against Liverpool, when they led 3–0 at half time yet lost in a penalty shoot-out. Their attempt to start to put that devastating memory behind them was failing as Fenerbahçe held them 1–1 at home with a few minutes left, but then Kaká took command.

Collecting Massimo Ambrosini's pass, he used strength to shrug off Serkan Balci, who ended up on the floor, dummied Fábio Luciano and skipped outside Ümit Özat before sliding the ball home. Two years later he was named FIFA World Player of the Year, the eighth time in 14 seasons that the award had gone to a Brazilian.

"It was like a goal from another era. Ricky is the only player capable of doing something like that in the modern game" **Milan coach Carlo Ancelotti**

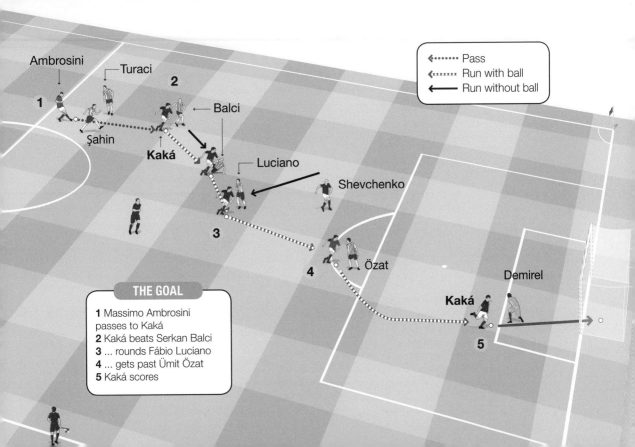

Ambrosini

Turaci

1

2

Şahin

Kaká

Balci

Luciano

Shevchenko

3

4

Özat

Demirel

Kaká

5

Pass

Run with ball

Run without ball

THE GOAL

1 Massimo Ambrosini
passes to Kaká
2 Kaká beats Serkan Balci
3 ... rounds Fábio Luciano
4 ... gets past Ümit Özat
5 Kaká scores

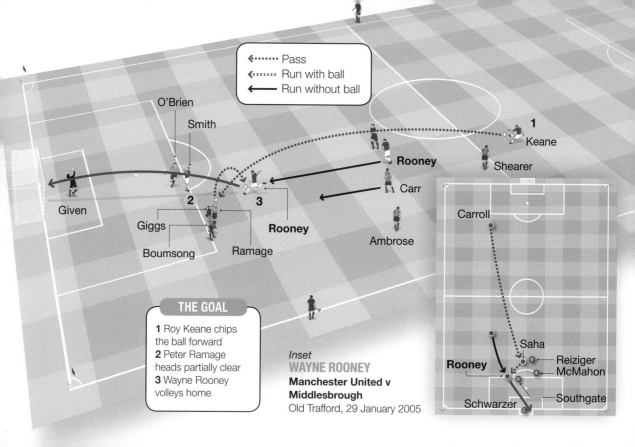

Pass
Run with ball
Run without ball

O'Brien

Smith

1
Keane

Rooney

Shearer

Given

Rooney

Carr

2

3

Giggs

Boumsong

Ramage

Rooney

Ambrose

Carroll

THE GOAL

1 Roy Keane chips
the ball forward
2 Peter Ramage
heads partially clear
3 Wayne Rooney
volleys home

Inset
WAYNE ROONEY
**Manchester United v
Middlesbrough**
Old Trafford, 29 January 2005

Saha

Rooney

Reiziger

McMahon

Southgate

Schwarzer

060 WAYNE ROONEY
Manchester United v Newcastle United,
24 April 2005 The instant hit

It was the perfect illustration of the young Wayne Rooney's standing in English football. Manchester United, the country's dominant club for the past 12 years, were enduring a disappointing season and relying on a teenager to keep them in the hunt for trophies. And in this game against Newcastle United, make that an injured teenager.

United were heading for a third league defeat in a row with around half an hour left and Rooney was about to be substituted because of a dead leg. As if anxious to make a mark quickly before he was hauled off, he advanced to meet a clearing header and – without breaking stride or pausing to size up the shot – thundered a swerving volley into the net from long distance.

That equaliser rescued United, who had not scored for more than six hours but who were now inspired to grab a victory. It was Rooney's sixteenth goal of the season and, aptly, he was named PFA Young Player of the Year later that day. The youngster's volley, square on to goal, was reminiscent of his strike three months earlier against Middlesbrough in the FA Cup, which also came at the Stretford End.

United manager Sir Alex Ferguson had splashed out £30 million to take Rooney from Everton at the start of the season, an apparent extravagance having spent a combined £20 million for two other strikers – Louis Saha and Alan Smith – in the previous seven months. But it sometimes pays to seize the moment, as Rooney showed against Newcastle.

THE MATCH

English league
Old Trafford

Manchester United 2
Rooney 57, Brown 75
Newcastle United 1
Ambrose 27
Att: 67,845

"It was an absolutely fantastic goal, especially considering he was injured" Manchester United manager Sir Alex Ferguson

061 GUS POYET
Chelsea v Sunderland, 7 August 1999
The impudent tee-up

The sun shone brightly and Chelsea optimism abounded. Fresh from finishing third in the league the previous season, their highest position since 1970, they faced Sunderland on the opening day of the next campaign with a squad reinforced by the signings of Didier Deschamps, a World Cup winner with France a year earlier, and Chris Sutton, a prolific goalscorer.

A 4-0 success further encouraged those tipping them for the league title, especially as the victory was rounded off in brilliant fashion. Gus Poyet, a Uruguayan midfielder, had headed the first goal and set up Gianfranco Zola for the second; now the pair combined for the memorable fourth.

A long ball from Deschamps was controlled expertly on the volley by Zola, who then waited as Poyet started a run from ten yards behind him. When his team-mate was level with him, the Italian chipped the ball perfectly over Sunderland's backline and into the path of Poyet, who, sneaking between Steve Bould and Michael Gray as he entered the penalty area, leapt high to volley joyously into the net from square on.

It was a cerebral goal produced by two foreign players who would later pursue managerial careers in England. Back in the 1999–2000 season however, they could not help Chelsea sustain a title challenge – while Deschamps impressed, Sutton struggled – but at least they enjoyed an FA Cup triumph as a reward for their artistry.

THE MATCH

English league
Stamford Bridge

Chelsea 4
Poyet 20, Zola 32,
Flo 77, Poyet 78
Sunderland 0
Att: 34,831

"He waited [to pass] because he knew his qualities would give him a chance to put the ball over all the defenders for me to finish and he knew that I would keep running" Gus Poyet on Gianfranco Zola

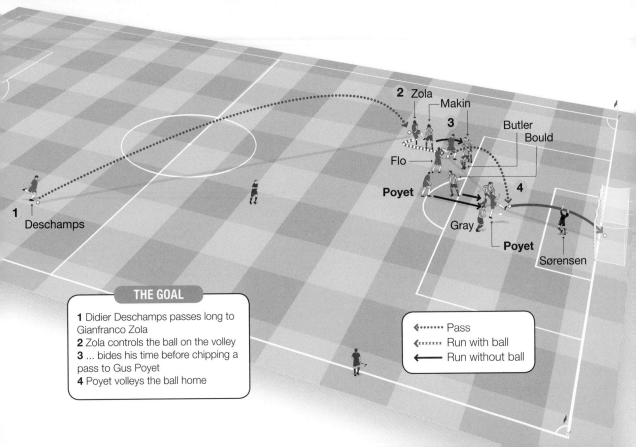

2 Zola

Makin

3

Butler
Bould

Flo

Poyet

4

1
Deschamps

Gray

Poyet

Sørensen

THE GOAL

1 Didier Deschamps passes long to
Gianfranco Zola
2 Zola controls the ball on the volley
3 ... bides his time before chipping a
pass to Gus Poyet
4 Poyet volleys the ball home

◀••••••• Pass
◀▪▪▪▪▪▪▪ Run with ball
◀━━━━━ Run without ball

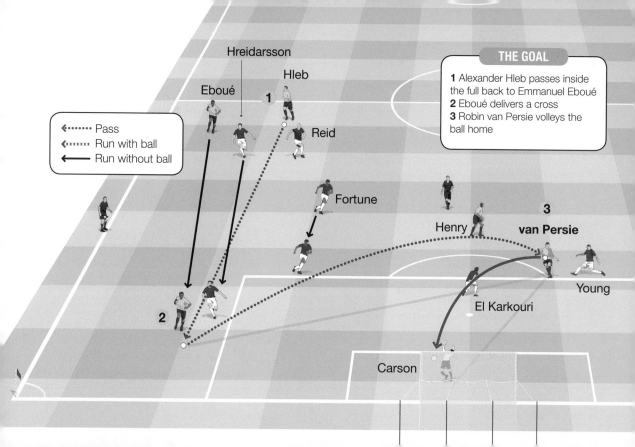

Hreidarsson

Hleb

Eboué

1

Reid

···· Pass
···· Run with ball
— Run without ball

THE GOAL

1 Alexander Hleb passes inside the full back to Emmanuel Eboué
2 Eboué delivers a cross
3 Robin van Persie volleys the ball home

Fortune

Henry

3

van Persie

2

El Karkouri

Young

Carson

062 ROBIN VAN PERSIE
Charlton Athletic v Arsenal, 30 September 2006
The cross and crash

At Dennis Bergkamp's testimonial match two months earlier Arsenal fans had bid farewell to one great Dutch striker, and here they acclaimed another. Robin van Persie had yet to establish himself fully in the two years since he arrived in North London but this spectacular volley brought hope that he might eventually match the influence of his compatriot.

Previously in this game van Persie had not resembled a player who might soon produce a moment of magic. He sent a free-kick too high, was slightly lucky to avoid a red card for kicking Jimmy Floyd Hasselbaink and incurred the wrath of team-mate Thierry Henry by shooting wildly when he should probably have passed to the Frenchman.

Yet it was van Persie who scored to cancel out Darren Bent's effort for Charlton Athletic and then added Arsenal's second goal in spectacular style. As Emmanuel Eboué's right-wing cross floated towards him, the Dutchman's path to goal was blocked by Luke Young's outstretched foot so he was required to leap high to guide the ball skilfully and powerfully into the roof of the net.

It was the perfect present for Arsenal manager Arsène Wenger, who was a day short of his tenth anniversary at the club, but in subsequent years Wenger would curse van Persie's frequent unavailability. In fact, given his injury record, it was brave of the striker to mark the goal against Charlton by dancing on an advertising board. Four months later he ended his season prematurely by fracturing a metatarsal when celebrating a goal against Manchester United.

"It was the goal of a lifetime" Arsenal manager Arsène Wenger

063 MANICHE
Portugal v Holland, 30 June 2004
The curler from the corner

When Maniche was dropped from Portugal's squad by manager Luiz Felipe Scolari for supposedly not trying hard enough in a friendly defeat by Spain in September 2003, he seemed unlikely to be selected for the European championship the following summer. "Sometimes I have to play the role of a father who punishes his children," Scolari said by way of explanation.

But the manager ended the 9-month exile by recalling Maniche for the tournament and starting him in all six of Portugal's matches. The energetic Porto midfielder responded by playing a key role in their progress as they became only the third host country since 1978 to reach the final of a World Cup or European championship.

Portugal's stylish approach to playing the game had earned them the nickname 'Brazilians of Europe', and the image was reinforced by the presence of Scolari, who had led his native Brazil to a World Cup triumph two years earlier. Moreover, the decisive goal in the semi-final victory over Holland, which took Portugal to their first ever major final, had a distinctively Brazilian flavour.

A corner taken short on Portugal's left by Cristiano Ronaldo gave Maniche the space to advance to the edge of the penalty area. From there he delivered a thunderous shot that bent dramatically on an inward curve around three Dutchmen, including Edwin van der Sar, the goalkeeper, and cannoned into the net off the far post. The disciplinarian father watched on proudly from the sidelines.

"Seeing as van der Sar is a tall goalkeeper, I knew that the only spot where he did not have a chance was the top corner" Maniche

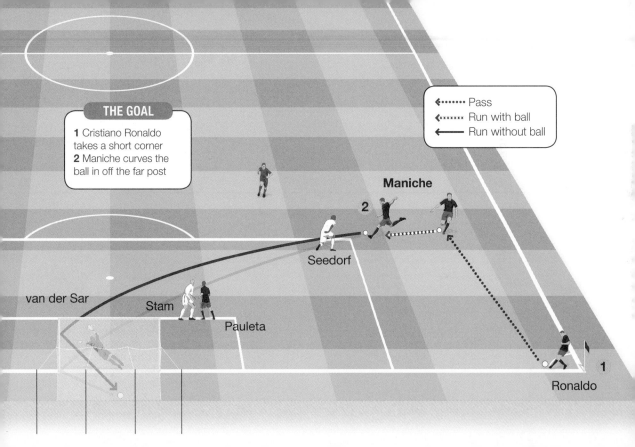

THE GOAL

1 Cristiano Ronaldo takes a short corner
2 Maniche curves the ball in off the far post

→······· Pass
→:::::: Run with ball
→——— Run without ball

Maniche

2

Seedorf

van der Sar

Stam

Pauleta

Ronaldo

1

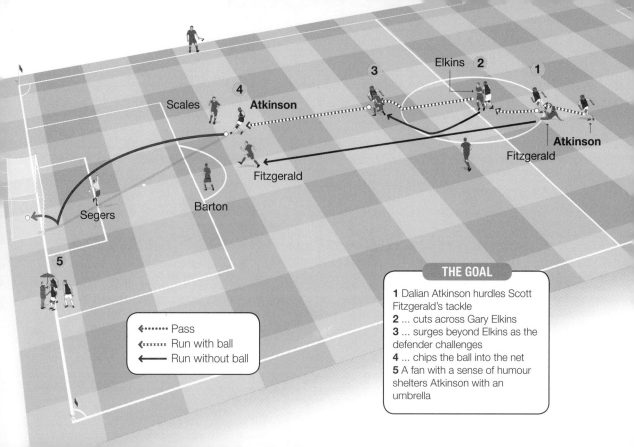

Elkins **2** **1**

3

Scales **4**

Atkinson

Atkinson

Fitzgerald

Fitzgerald

Segers

Barton

5

Pass ◀·······
Run with ball ◀┅┅┅
Run without ball ◀━━━

THE GOAL

1 Dalian Atkinson hurdles Scott Fitzgerald's tackle
2 ... cuts across Gary Elkins
3 ... surges beyond Elkins as the defender challenges
4 ... chips the ball into the net
5 A fan with a sense of humour shelters Atkinson with an umbrella

064 DALIAN ATKINSON
Wimbledon v Aston Villa, 3 October 1992
The waltz in the wet

Vinnie Jones, the tough-tackling Wimbledon midfielder, had caused a furore in the week before this game by bringing out a video in which violent challenges were glorified. Coincidentally – or perhaps not, given the frequency of his disciplinary problems – Jones was starting a three-game ban for a red card against Blackburn Rovers when his team faced Aston Villa. His absence was just as well, otherwise Dalian Atkinson might have been hacked to the ground rather than be allowed to run 50 yards to score a memorable goal.

Villa rose to fifth in the Premier League table with this third league win in a row, a sequence in which they scored ten goals and conceded six. They were playing with an abandon that was typified by Atkinson's decision to embark on an ambitious dribble from inside his own half rather than play safe to protect his team's 2-1 lead.

The striker's ability to run with the ball at great speed had persuaded Ron Atkinson, the manager and his namesake, to sign him twice, first to take him to Sheffield Wednesday and later to Villa. The player demonstrated this gift at Selhurst Park when he powered past Scott Fitzgerald and Gary Elkins, the latter twice, before chipping the ball deftly over Hans Segers, the goalkeeper.

As Atkinson stood in front of the Villa fans, arms outstretched as if checking the goal met with their approval, one spectator ran on to the pitch with an umbrella to shield his hero from the rain. But it was the Wimbledon defence who had needed protection.

THE MATCH

English league
Selhurst Park

Wimbledon 2
Miller 34, Clarke 90
Aston Villa 3
Saunders 5, Saunders 29,
Atkinson 77
Att: 6,849

"He scores hundreds like that [in training]. I've tried to stop him doing that" **Aston Villa manager Ron Atkinson**

065 ALAN MULLERY
Fulham v Leicester City, 26 January 1974
The jabbed volley

Many leading players chose to wind down their careers by the Thames in the 1970s. Bobby Moore, George Best and Rodney Marsh all experienced life outside the top division in the tranquil and homely surroundings of Fulham but Alan Mullery was the first of the quartet to do so, moving there in 1972 shortly after helping Tottenham Hotspur to win the UEFA Cup.

It might seem surprising that Mullery dropped a division less than a year after winning his 35th and final England cap, but it was an understandable destination, as Fulham had given him his first league appearance 15 years earlier. Furthermore, born in London, he never played for or managed an English club north of the capital: he took charge of Brighton and Hove Albion,

Charlton Athletic, Crystal Palace, Queens Park Rangers and Barnet.

Before the match against Leicester City few Fulham fans would have considered Mullery a likely goalscorer given that he had managed just two goals in 31 games that season. But soon after kick-off, when Barry Lloyd's diagonal ball found him on the edge of the D, he needed no time to set his sights, smashing a volley first-time into the corner of the net without breaking stride. The suddenness of the shot meant Peter Shilton, the goalkeeper, dived too late.

Leicester recovered to equalise and win the replay, but Mullery and Fulham fared better the next season when they reached the final. Mullery, though, did not score another FA Cup goal after this one. What a way to sign off.

"My big points are hard tackles and lots of energy"
Alan Mullery, revealing he was not characterised by eye-catching goals such as this

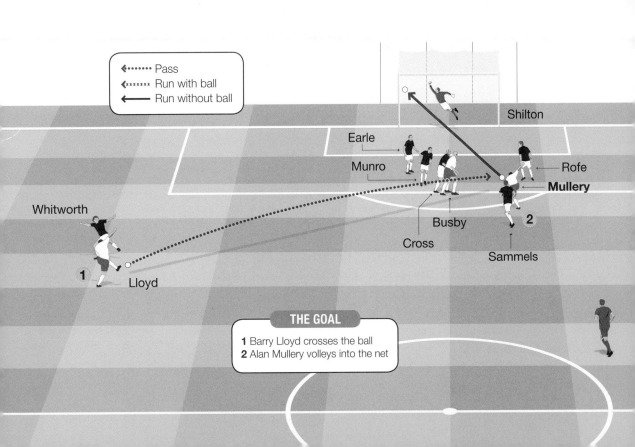

Pass
Run with ball
Run without ball

Shilton

Earle

Munro

Rofe

Mullery

Busby

Cross

Sammels

Whitworth

1

Lloyd

2

THE GOAL

1 Barry Lloyd crosses the ball
2 Alan Mullery volleys into the net

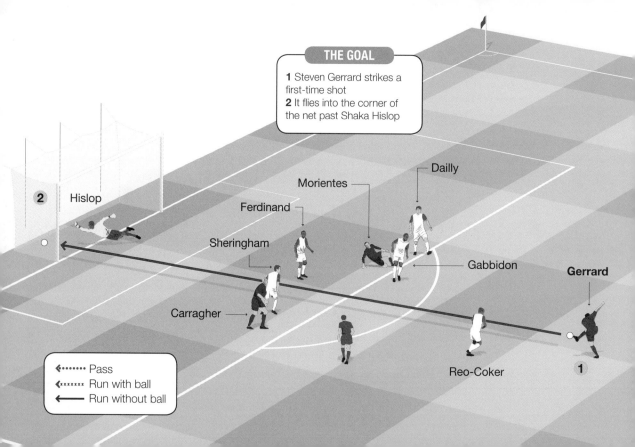

THE GOAL

1 Steven Gerrard strikes a first-time shot
2 It flies into the corner of the net past Shaka Hislop

2 Hislop

Dailly

Morientes

Ferdinand

Sheringham

Gabbidon

Carragher

Gerrard

Reo-Coker

1

Pass

Run with ball

Run without ball

066 STEVEN GERRARD
Liverpool v West Ham United, 13 May 2006
The 35-yard rocket

One obvious threat remained to West Ham United's hopes of lifting the FA Cup in 2006 as they held a 3–2 lead with stoppage time approaching. Steven Gerrard was Liverpool's captain, energiser and leading scorer and had shown his ability to drag his team back from the brink in a final 12 months earlier when they recovered from 3–0 down to draw 3–3 with AC Milan in the Champions League, which his team won in a penalty shoot-out.

Furthermore, as a loose ball fell near Gerrard centrally and outside the penalty area, the mind's eye could see him striking two important goals from a similar position: a drive that put England ahead in their 5–1 World Cup qualifying win away to Germany in 2001 and a late effort against Olympiacos

that sent Liverpool through to the Champions League knock-out phase at the expense of their opponents in 2004–05.

Yet those goals were eclipsed for skill and drama here. Quick-thinking and dynamic yet suffering from cramp, Gerrard saw the ball bounce towards him 35 yards out and, in a flash, smashed it through a crowd of players low into the corner of the net.

It was the last of his 23 goals from midfield that season, ten more than he had managed in any previous campaign for Liverpool, although he added a successful penalty as his team won the FA Cup in a shoot-out. Any West Ham players whose vote helped Gerrard to become PFA Player of the Year that season would have acknowledged ruefully that their assessment had been justified.

"Gerrard doesn't know when he's beaten"
Alan Hansen, TV analyst and former Liverpool player

067 ESTEBAN CAMBIASSO

Argentina v Serbia and Montenegro, 16 June 2006
The patient wait and pounce

On the eve of this match José Pekerman revealed why he had dropped Esteban Cambiasso from his Argentina side and picked Lucho González instead. He wanted quick, creative passing and Cambiasso, a defensive midfielder, was considered a good tackler but ponderous.

After the game Pekerman predictably did not raise the subject again. Cambiasso, an early substitute when González suffered an injury, soon played a key part in one of the World Cup's greatest passing movements. It was he, despite his coach's concerns, who moved the ball into the Serbia and Montenegro penalty area and who burst forward to apply the finishing touch.

Argentina had succumbed in a difficult group at the 2002 World Cup and here, in Germany, some fans feared a repeat after another tough draw. But they booked their place in the knock-out phase when victory over Ivory Coast was followed by this thrashing of a team that had conceded only two goals in 12 competitive games.

Argentina's second goal featured 24 passes, 20 of them patient and 4 brilliantly incisive. Those last four started with Juan Román Riquelme's return ball to Javier Saviola, who passed first-time to Cambiasso. The latter found Hernán Crespo, whose back-heel teed up Cambiasso to score. In the VIP seats in Gelsenkirchen there were wild celebrations from Diego Maradona, who had scored a classic individual goal for Argentina against England at the 1986 World Cup. Here, though, it was decidedly a team effort.

"It was a beautiful goal and I am proud to have played a part in it"
Hernán Crespo

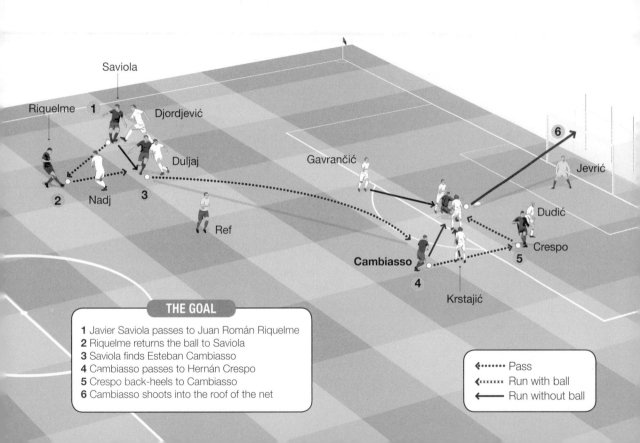

Saviola

Riquelme **1**

Djordjević

Duljaj

Gavrančić

6

Jevrić

2

Nadj

3

Dudić

Ref

Cambiasso

Crespo

5

4

Krstajić

THE GOAL

1 Javier Saviola passes to Juan Román Riquelme
2 Riquelme returns the ball to Saviola
3 Saviola finds Esteban Cambiasso
4 Cambiasso passes to Hernán Crespo
5 Crespo back-heels to Cambiasso
6 Cambiasso shoots into the roof of the net

←······· Pass
←:::::::: Run with ball
←———— Run without ball

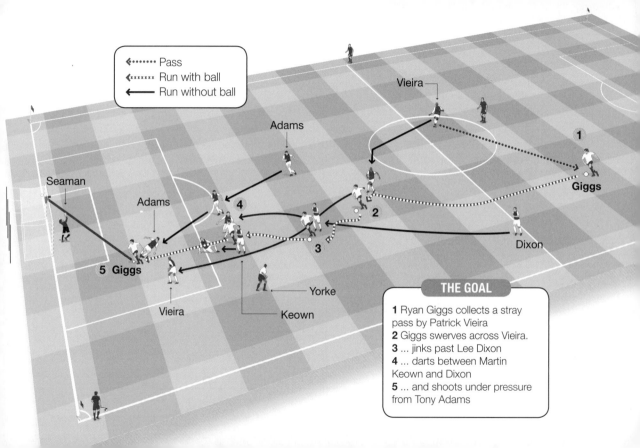

Pass ⬅┄┄┄
Run with ball ⬅┄┄┄
Run without ball ⬅━━━

Vieira

1

Giggs

Adams

4

Adams

Seaman

2

Dixon

3

5 Giggs

Vieira

Yorke

Keown

THE GOAL

1 Ryan Giggs collects a stray pass by Patrick Vieira
2 Giggs swerves across Vieira.
3 ... jinks past Lee Dixon
4 ... darts between Martin Keown and Dixon
5 ... and shoots under pressure from Tony Adams

068 RYAN GIGGS
Manchester United v Arsenal, 14 April 1999
The wavy run

"He floated over the ground like a cocker spaniel chasing a piece of silver paper in the wind." A 13-year-old Ryan Giggs inspired that poetic thought from Sir Alex Ferguson, and how the Manchester United manager benefited from that graceful movement when the Welsh winger ascended to the first team.

Giggs adapted his playing style as his incredible two-decade career matured, but dribbling at pace was his early trademark. He made his name before he turned 21 by scoring two goals – away to Tottenham Hotspur and Queens Park Rangers – in which he took on the opposing defence single-handedly and at high speed. His most famous strike came in a similar manner against different opponents from London.

Such were the circumstances of the match, the last FA Cup semi-final replay, that Giggs's goal against Arsenal would have been momentous had it been a mere tap-in. United, hanging on after Roy Keane's 74th-minute dismissal, had given away a stoppage-time penalty only for Peter Schmeichel to save Dennis Bergkamp's effort, sending England's best two teams into extra-time. Traditionalists who regret the scrapping of semi-final replays cite this game as a fine example of the system working.

When Giggs began his run in his own half, Ferguson was urging the player to "take it to the corner flag" to waste time and earn a penalty shoot-out. Instead Giggs evaded all challenges and smashed his shot past David Seaman. The spaniel was unleashed and untouchable.

"I went on that run because I was having a dreadful game. In situations like that I always try and dribble" Ryan Giggs

069 ALAN SHEARER
Newcastle United v Everton, 1 December 2002
The piledriver with poise

The minutes ticked down in the contest between the immovable object and the irresistible force. On one hand Everton had won their previous five Premier League games 1–0 and were heading for a sixth. On the other were Newcastle United, battering away at their opponents having come from behind for victory in three of their previous four home league games. The latter, with Alan Shearer in their ranks, would prevail.

Shearer was the greatest goalscorer of his generation: he struck 260 goals in the Premier League whereas no other player reached 200 in the competition's first 20 years. He had retired from England duty in 2000 at the age of 29 to prolong his Newcastle career, and, while his pace was starting to slow, he did not need it for this goal.

Eight months earlier Everton had lost 6–2 at St James' Park and they might have conceded another six here, yet they clung to a lead for more than an hour after losing Joseph Yobo to a 22nd-minute red card. Then, with four minutes left, Laurent Robert's long ball was headed sideways by Shola Ameobi and Shearer smashed his shot home on the volley from 25 yards.

Three minutes later Craig Bellamy's effort was deflected into his own goal by Everton's Li Tie and Newcastle's Shearer-inspired turnaround was complete. His home-town club had signed him for a world record £15 million in 1996, and this was yet another afternoon when the enormous fee seemed more than justified.

"You won't see anything better than that because it was a perfect strike. It was a blur as it went past the goalkeeper"
Newcastle manager Sir Bobby Robson

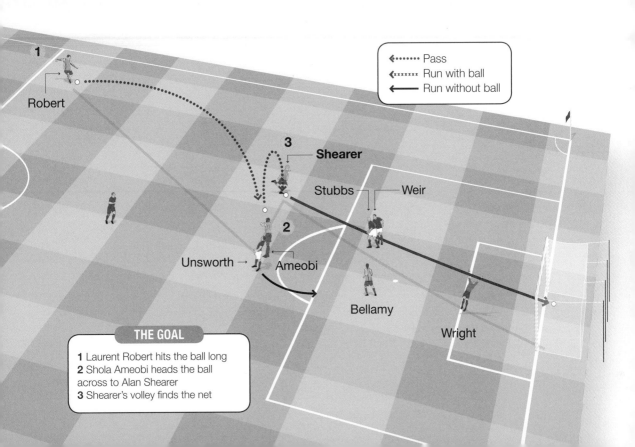

← ⋯⋯ Pass
← ⋯⋯⋯ Run with ball
← ——— Run without ball

1

Robert

3

Shearer

Stubbs   Weir

2

Unsworth →   Ameobi

Bellamy

Wright

THE GOAL

1 Laurent Robert hits the ball long
2 Shola Ameobi heads the ball
across to Alan Shearer
3 Shearer's volley finds the net

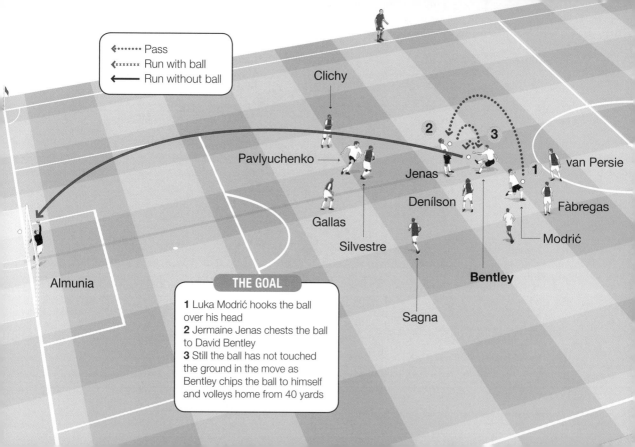

Pass
Run with ball
Run without ball

Clichy

Pavlyuchenko

2

3

van Persie

Jenas

Gallas

Denílson

Silvestre

Modrić

Fàbregas

Almunia

Bentley

1

Sagna

THE GOAL

1 Luka Modrić hooks the ball over his head
2 Jermaine Jenas chests the ball to David Bentley
3 Still the ball has not touched the ground in the move as Bentley chips the ball to himself and volleys home from 40 yards

070 DAVID BENTLEY

Arsenal v Tottenham Hotspur, 29 October 2008
The 40-yard volley

The booing was a familiar sound to David Bentley. The Tottenham Hotspur winger was jeered in this match by Arsenal fans who recalled his stint at their club, when he complained he was not picked in the team enough. Eight months before this game he was booed by the Wembley crowd on his England debut, this time for the opposite reason – his country's under-21 side had selected him for a tournament but he had refused to play, citing the need to rest.

An outspoken character, he had also criticised his treatment by Tottenham since arriving from Blackburn Rovers that summer for a £15 million transfer fee. He had struggled for form and blamed Juande Ramos, the manager, for playing him out of position on the left of midfield. But

Ramos was sacked and replaced by Harry Redknapp, who returned Bentley to his customary position on the right.

Bentley's star had risen so high at Blackburn that David Beckham was no longer a unanimous choice for the title of best England right-winger named David B. Now, in Redknapp's second game in charge, with Tottenham starting to improve after their decline under Ramos, the player produced a reminder of his talents.

Standing 40 yards from goal, he chipped the ball to himself and surprised most onlookers, including Manuel Almunia, by attempting a lob that the back-pedalling Arsenal goalkeeper could only palm into the net. Tottenham's dramatic late comeback to force a 4–4 draw meant Bentley's goal had proved significant. Arsenal supporters now had even more reason to dislike him.

"I feel like Superman, I could fly home" **David Bentley**

071 ROBERTO BAGGIO
Italy v Czechoslovakia, 19 June 1990
The winding road

So negative were teams at the 1990 World Cup that FIFA were persuaded to change the rules in favour of attacking and creative players. By the time the trophy was contested again four years later, goalkeepers were prohibited from handling back passes and fouls earned far stiffer punishments. A tournament of ill-discipline and a record-low 2.21 goals per game had forced the world governing body to act.

At least there was Roberto Baggio to lift the spirits. Italy, the hosts, had helped set the tone by playing cautiously in their opening group games. In fact, after uninspiring performances in the meetings with Austria and the United States, they were heading for a third consecutive 1–0 victory when

Baggio conjured up a brilliant solo goal late on against Czechoslovakia that captured the imagination of the nation.

Fiorentina fans were certainly aware of Baggio's gifts: many of them rioted when he left them for Juventus a month before the World Cup began. Italy coach Azeglio Vicini was apparently not quite so convinced of his talents, leaving him on the bench for the first two games before throwing him in against Czechoslovakia.

Vicini was rewarded when the player collected the ball on the halfway line, played a one-two with Giuseppe Giannini, hurdled one challenge and skipped round another before sliding the ball home. It was the first of nine goals for Baggio that were spread across three World Cups. At Italia '90, the pulse was quickening at last.

"Still Baggio. Oh, yes ... oh, yes ... oh, yes"
TV commentator Alan Parry

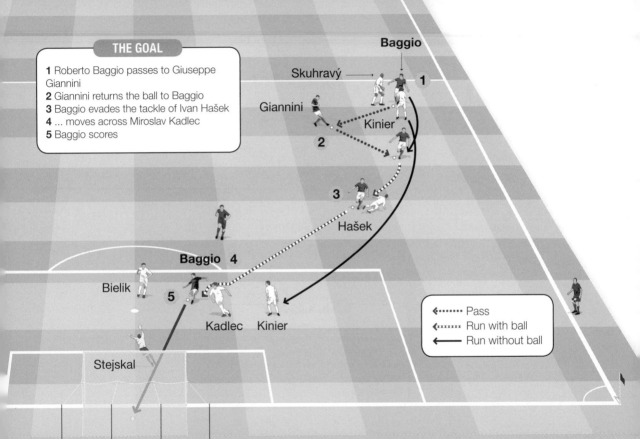

THE GOAL

1 Roberto Baggio passes to Giuseppe Giannini
2 Giannini returns the ball to Baggio
3 Baggio evades the tackle of Ivan Hašek
4 ... moves across Miroslav Kadlec
5 Baggio scores

Baggio

Skuhravý →

Giannini

Kinier

2

3

Hašek

Baggio **4**

Bielik

5

Kadlec   Kinier

Stejskal

◀······· Pass
◀∷∷∷∷ Run with ball
◀———— Run without ball

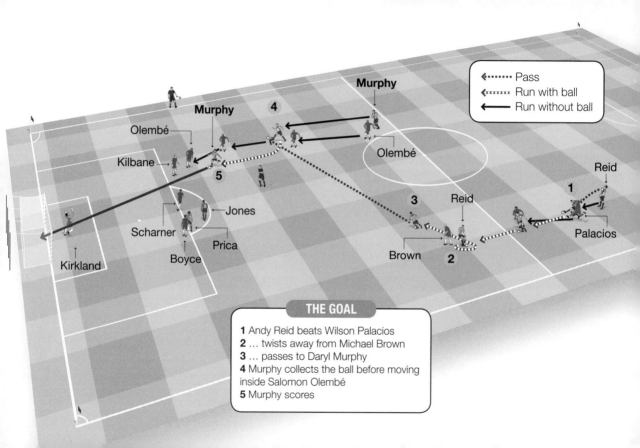

Murphy

Murphy

Olembé

Kilbane

Olembé

5

4

Reid

3

Reid

1

Scharner → Jones

Prica

Boyce

Brown

Palacios

2

Kirkland

- - - - - - → Pass
- - - - - - → Run with ball
━━━━━━ Run without ball

THE GOAL

1 Andy Reid beats Wilson Palacios
2 … twists away from Michael Brown
3 … passes to Daryl Murphy
4 Murphy collects the ball before moving inside Salomon Olembé
5 Murphy scores

072 DARYL MURPHY
Sunderland v Wigan Athletic, 9 February 2008
The audacious attack

When Andy Reid became the eighth fellow-Irishman to be signed by Roy Keane just 17 months after the latter became Sunderland manager, it invited scepticism among the team's fans. Reid, whose rotund shape made him an easy target, had rarely impressed at Tottenham Hotspur and had then suffered relegation with Charlton Athletic. The main reason he had been brought to the Stadium of Light was his nationality, so the theory went.

If Reid felt he needed to prove himself quickly at his new club, that is exactly what happened. His first contribution just seconds after emerging for his debut against Wigan Athletic was to beat two opponents and supply an audacious, cross-field pass. Aptly enough, the ball was collected and smashed into the net from long range by Daryl Murphy, another Irishman.

Sunderland sat close to the relegation zone but possessed a split personality. The no-hopers who had lost their previous nine away league games were transformed when playing at home, where they extended their winning league run to four by seeing off Wigan. The confidence they exuded at the Stadium of Light was evident in Murphy's goal.

Reid, a late substitute, took the ball past Wilson Palacios with his first touches, spun away from Michael Brown near the halfway line and drove a long, low pass perfectly inside Salomon Olembé and into the path of Murphy. The forward cut across Olembé and found the roof of the net from 25 yards out. Wigan twice hit the woodwork but the home side prevailed. A case of the luck of the Irish?

"The first 30 seconds was okay, I suppose!"
Andy Reid on his dramatic first touches in a Sunderland shirt

073 GIANFRANCO ZOLA
Chelsea v Norwich City, 16 January 2002
The side-flick stab

Gianfranco Zola was a late developer, plucked from lower-division Italian league football in his native Sardinia at 23 to experience his first taste of the top flight with Napoli. But he was able to make up for lost time by observing and copying the club's star player so effectively that he was soon known as the "new Maradona", a comparison encouraged by their equally short stature.

Then, when Diego Maradona left Napoli in 1991, Zola took on the Argentine's mantle. Creative but combative, he was two-footed and possessed a great technique. He would continue to defy the conventions of age by giving Chelsea seven wonderful years after signing at 30.

Now 35, he had recently been dropped for ten games by Chelsea so, when Norwich City visited Stamford Bridge for an FA Cup replay, he was perhaps determined to show he was not over the hill. He certainly demonstrated that, although his team's easy victory was no foregone conclusion beforehand. Their inconsistent form had led to them being outplayed by Norwich, a second-tier side, in the goalless first match.

When Graeme Le Saux's corner located Zola at the near post after he had run across the penalty area to meet the cross, the Italian side-flicked the ball with his right foot on the volley, sending it behind his left leg and into the net. A replay on the stadium's big screen drew a round of applause as spectators took in the full wizardry of the shot. It was a goal of which even Maradona would have been proud.

THE MATCH

FA Cup third round replay
Stamford Bridge

Chelsea 4
Stanić 11, Lampard 56, Zola 63, Forssell 89
Norwich City 0
Att: 24,231

"You have to try crazy things to make them come true. You can't really think about it, you just have to do it" Gianfranco Zola

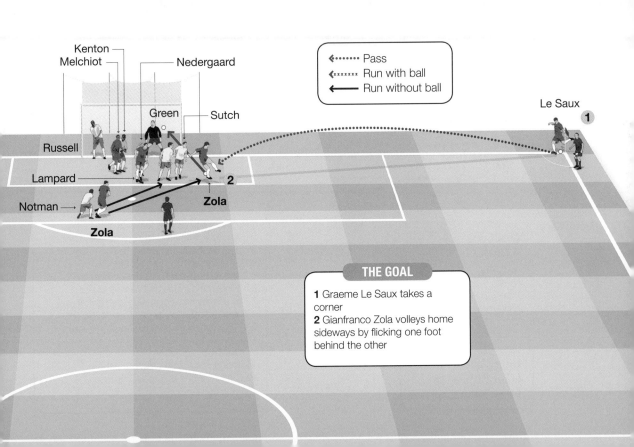

Kenton
Melchiot
Nedergaard

Green — Sutch

Le Saux
①

Russell

Lampard

Notman → **Zola** 2
Zola

←······· Pass
←······· Run with ball
←——— Run without ball

THE GOAL

1 Graeme Le Saux takes a corner
2 Gianfranco Zola volleys home sideways by flicking one foot behind the other

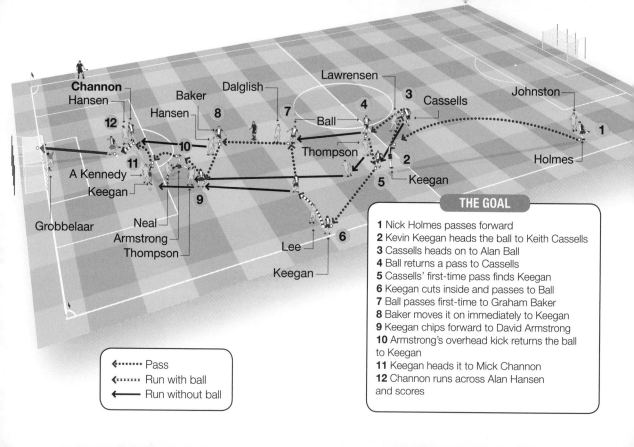

Channon
Hansen

12

Hansen

Baker

8

Dalglish

7

Lawrensen

3

Cassells

Johnston

1

Ball

4

10

A Kennedy

11

Thompson

Keegan

2

Holmes

Keegan

5

Keegan

9

Grobbelaar

Neal
Armstrong
Thompson

Lee

6

Keegan

THE GOAL

1 Nick Holmes passes forward
2 Kevin Keegan heads the ball to Keith Cassells
3 Cassells heads on to Alan Ball
4 Ball returns a pass to Cassells
5 Cassells' first-time pass finds Keegan
6 Keegan cuts inside and passes to Ball
7 Ball passes first-time to Graham Baker
8 Baker moves it on immediately to Keegan
9 Keegan chips forward to David Armstrong
10 Armstrong's overhead kick returns the ball
to Keegan
11 Keegan heads it to Mick Channon
12 Channon runs across Alan Hansen
and scores

◆······· Pass
◆······· Run with ball
◆—— Run without ball

074 MICK CHANNON
Southampton v Liverpool, 24 April 1982
The one-touch wonder

It was one of the biggest transfer surprises in English football. Kevin Keegan, winner of the previous two European Player of the Year awards, was leaving Hamburg for Southampton, who had never finished above seventh in the league. The move attracted him, he explained, partly because he would be linking up with Mick Channon, his best friend in football.

In their first season together, 1980–81, the two forwards helped Southampton to a new highest finishing position of sixth. As the following campaign reached the home straight they were in fifth when they faced Liverpool with Keegan, 31, and Channon, 33, joined by another England veteran in Alan Ball, 36. The trio all contributed to this brilliant short-passing move.

Liverpool had won their previous nine league games but Southampton – who would draw their next home match 5–5 against Coventry City – were playing with a freedom that made them veer from vulnerable to irresistible. For this goal they made 11 passes from the moment Nick Holmes played the ball forward from left back, seven of them struck first-time, four by Keegan and one by Ball.

The last of those by Keegan, a header, set up Channon, who cut across Alan Hansen to score what would prove the last of his 185 league goals for Southampton, which remained a club record three decades later. Not that his sporting partnership with his friend was over. Years later, as a successful trainer, he took charge of a racehorse that was owned by Keegan.

THE MATCH

**English league
The Dell**

Southampton 2
Channon 37,
Keegan pen. 58
Liverpool 3
Rush 12, Whelan 57,
Whelan 88
Att: 24,704

"Our defence usually at least gets in the way of attacks but this one we just didn't even see" Liverpool defender Phil Thompson

075 PAUL GASCOIGNE
England v Scotland, 15 June 1996
The dink and volley

The Euro 96 slogan was "Football Comes Home" because England, who formulated the rules of the game, were hosting their first major tournament for 30 years. But "Gascoigne Comes Home" would also have been apt. The midfielder was widely considered his country's finest player for a generation, but English audiences had been deprived of seeing him in the flesh.

Gascoigne had made just five competitive appearances on English soil in five years – all for his country – since his time as a Tottenham Hotspur player ended. Spells at Lazio and Rangers followed, and when he eventually returned to his home country in 1998, now in his thirties, it was only to play in the second tier with Middlesbrough.

The meeting with Scotland was the first since the fixture had been halted because of hooliganism seven years before, so the resurrection of international football's oldest rivalry gave Gascoigne a platform firmly in the spotlight. He responded by scoring a remarkable goal, flicking the ball over Scotland defender Colin Hendry with his left foot and volleying the ball home with his right.

Just a minute earlier Scotland had missed a penalty that would have brought the scores level, so England's exhilaration was all the greater. In celebration, Gascoigne lay down as Alan Shearer grabbed a bottle and squirted water into his mouth – a reminder of the "dentist's chair" drinking game that the squad had played, controversially, on a pre-tournament tour. Gascoigne's brilliance left Wembley with thousands of toothy grins.

THE MATCH

European championship group game
Wembley

England 2
Shearer 53,
Gascoigne 79
Scotland 0
Att: 76,864

"That goal was sensational; it was vintage Gascoigne"
England manager Terry Venables

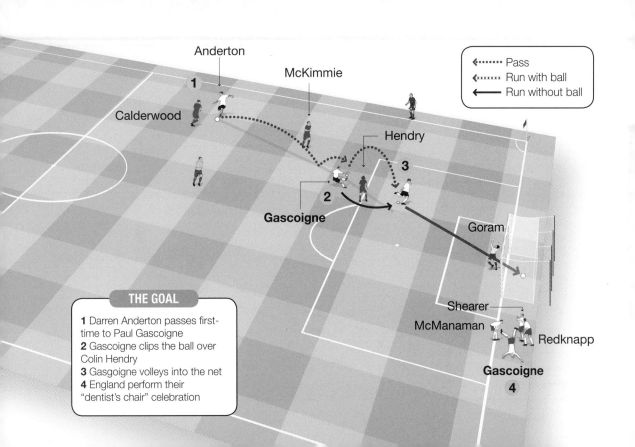

Anderton

McKimmie

Calderwood

Hendry

Gascoigne

Goram

Shearer

McManaman

Redknapp

Gascoigne

··········· Pass
······ Run with ball
Run without ball

THE GOAL

1 Darren Anderton passes first-time to Paul Gascoigne
2 Gascoigne clips the ball over Colin Hendry
3 Gascoigne volleys into the net
4 England perform their "dentist's chair" celebration

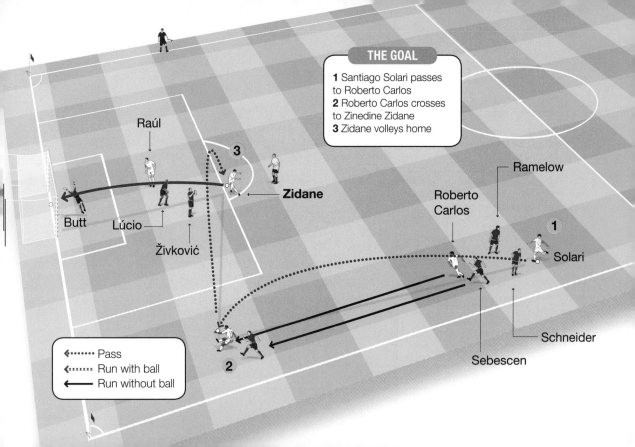

THE GOAL

1 Santiago Solari passes to Roberto Carlos
2 Roberto Carlos crosses to Zinedine Zidane
3 Zidane volleys home

Raúl

3

Zidane

Ramelow

Roberto
Carlos

1

Butt

Lúcio

Solari

Živković

Schneider

Sebescen

2

◀······· Pass
◀······· Run with ball
◀——— Run without ball

076 ZINEDINE ZIDANE
Real Madrid v Bayer Leverkusen, 15 May 2002
The pause and pirouette

Real Madrid are defined by their early monopoly of the European Cup. They won the first five tournaments from 1956 and ever since have been driven by their determination, or even expectation, that they will conquer the continent again soon. In their breathless pursuit of success they have sacked many unlucky managers: John Toshack, Vicente del Bosque and Fabio Capello, each after they won the Spanish title, Jupp Heynckes after his Champions League victory and Raddy Antić when his side led the league by seven points.

In 2002 the club's anxiety to celebrate their centenary in style intensified the pressure in the dressing room, as did the location of the Champions League final. Real met Bayer Leverkusen at Hampden Park, the setting for the club's most famous triumph in 1960 when they beat Eintracht Frankfurt, another German side, 7–3 to retain their European crown yet again.

With history weighing on their shoulders, Real leaned heavily on Zinedine Zidane, signed from Juventus the previous July for a world record £45.6 million, as they sought a record-extending ninth European title. The scores were level shortly before half-time when Roberto Carlos sent a high cross towards the Frenchman on the edge of the penalty area.

Zidane waited calmly for the ball to fall from the sky and swivelled as his left (weaker) foot sent a volley flying into the net. Real might believe that no player is bigger than the club, but the Frenchman came close to achieving such status on that night in Glasgow.

"It was so athletic, so beautiful" **Real Madrid coach Vicente del Bosque**

077 CESC FÀBREGAS
Arsenal v Tottenham Hotspur, 31 October 2009
The marauding run through the middle

Having made 151 appearances for Arsenal in his teens and become captain at just 21, Cesc Fàbregas was already revered by the club's fans. But here, still only 22, he enhanced his status even further – by joyously kicking bitter rivals Tottenham Hotspur when they were down.

Year after year during Arsène Wenger's reign at Arsenal the story was told that Tottenham were improving, that soon they would become the equals of their neighbours, but each time their hopes were dashed. Before the match Tottenham forward Robbie Keane claimed his club had built a stronger squad than that of Arsenal, who had not lost a North London derby in the league for ten years.

Arsenal had won all their eight home games that season but Tottenham's optimism abounded. Their outlook became less rosy when they fell behind just before the break and, as if to mock their foes' pretensions, the home side doubled their lead just 11 seconds after the restart. This second goal was a classic, though Fàbregas's brilliance was partially overlooked in the haste to criticise Tottenham's supposed lack of resolve.

The Spaniard collected a loose ball in midfield and his boldness, acceleration and close control took him clear of central midfielders Tom Huddlestone and Wilson Palacios. He then evaded Ledley King's lunge with nimble footwork before ignoring the attentions of Vedran Ćorluka and giving goalkeeper Heurelho Gomes no chance with a firm shot. In a flash the game, yet again, was up for Tottenham.

"Take your hat off to Cesc Fàbregas, he jumped all over Tottenham" **Andy Gray, TV commentator**

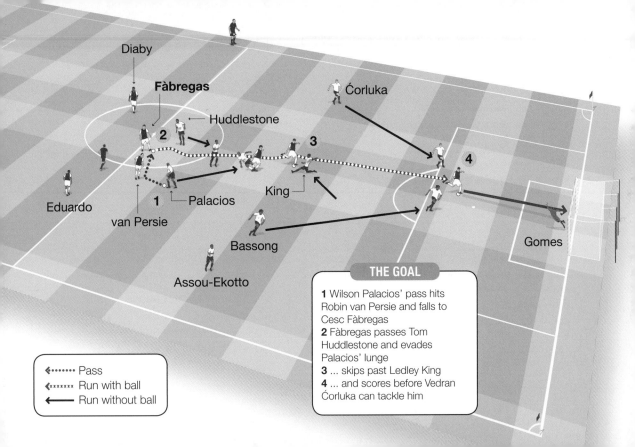

Diaby

Fàbregas

Huddlestone

Ćorluka

2

3

King

4

Eduardo

1

van Persie — Palacios

Bassong

Assou-Ekotto

Gomes

THE GOAL

1 Wilson Palacios' pass hits Robin van Persie and falls to Cesc Fàbregas

2 Fàbregas passes Tom Huddlestone and evades Palacios' lunge

3 ... skips past Ledley King

4 ... and scores before Vedran Ćorluka can tackle him

←······ Pass

←······ Run with ball

←—— Run without ball

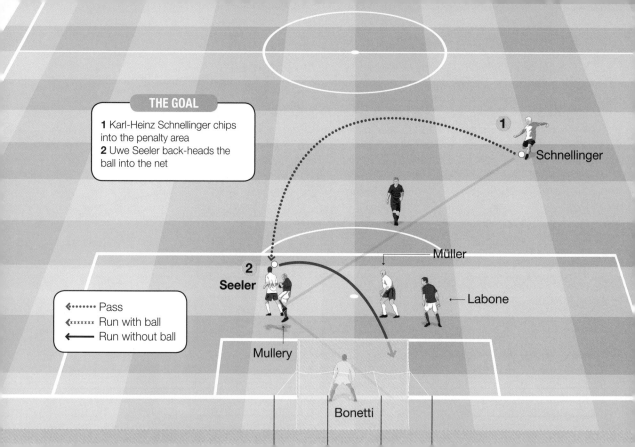

THE GOAL

1 Karl-Heinz Schnellinger chips into the penalty area
2 Uwe Seeler back-heads the ball into the net

1 Schnellinger

Müller

2
Seeler

Labone

◄······· Pass
◄······· Run with ball
◄——— Run without ball

Mullery

Bonetti

078 UWE SEELER
West Germany v England, 14 June 1970
The backwards header

If finding the net in front of you is usually harder when using your head rather than your feet, it is far trickier still when executing a backwards header to change the direction of the ball by 90 degrees. That is what Uwe Seeler achieved when scoring a goal that contributed to England's World Cup quarter-final collapse.

Not that everyone was impressed. One account claimed Seeler was aiming to head the ball across goal to Gerd Muller; another thought he was simply trying to keep the ball in play. But Seeler's history suggests it was deliberate. He was known for his unorthodox methods of scoring: he loved to attempt bicycle-kick shots and he once scored with a volley from 12 yards while lying on the ground.

Seeler certainly knew where the goal was, as this was the fourth World Cup in which he had scored, and he was recognised by the award of German Footballer of the Year in 1970. His late goal drew West Germany level at 2–2 as their opponents wilted in the lunchtime Mexican sun. Then, with England having substituted Bobby Charlton on his 106th appearance, which broke Billy Wright's cap record, the Germans scored an extra-time winner.

Criticism was focused on Peter Bonetti's uncertain performance in the England goal as a stand-in for the ill Gordon Banks, who was arguably the world's best in that position. Indeed, Bonetti was in no man's land when Seeler's header looped over him. But that should not detract from the German's inventive strike.

"An extraordinary goal" **Journalist and author Brian Glanville**

079 XABI ALONSO

Liverpool v Newcastle United, 20 September 2006

The shot from his own half

The Liverpool fan who, pre-season, bet £200 on Xabi Alonso scoring from his own half in the 2005–06 campaign had logic on his side. The Spaniard frequently hit passes of 50 or 60 yards accurately, so why was it such a long shot that he would succeed with a long shot? Odds of 125–1 were snapped up and winnings of £25,000 collected after the feat was achieved against Luton Town in an FA Cup third round match.

As if to prove it was no fluke, Alonso's next goal for Liverpool, against Newcastle United eight months later, was also struck from his own half. And as if to create variety, he used his left foot for the first goal, which dribbled over the line, and his right for the second, which flew straight into the net.

Alonso needed self-assurance. Rafael Benítez, the Liverpool manager, was about to tell off the midfielder for shooting instead of passing to Steven Gerrard against Newcastle. Gerrard was also well placed for a pass against Luton and waved his arms angrily at Alonso – before sheepishly changing his gesture to a clap as the ball rolled into the goal.

The Newcastle goal was more impressive. Whereas Alonso faced an open net against Luton because goalkeeper Marlon Beresford had yet to return after advancing when his team won a corner, the Spaniard's other goal saw him tackle Charles N'Zogbia and fire his effort over Steve Harper, the Newcastle goalkeeper, who slipped as he stretched in vain for the ball. The bookmakers hastily shortened their odds on it happening again.

THE MATCH

English league
Anfield

Liverpool 2
Kuyt 29, **Alonso 79**
Newcastle United 0
Att: 43,754

"I practise [long shots] all the time in training and sometimes the coaches shout at me for losing a lot of balls" **Xabi Alonso**

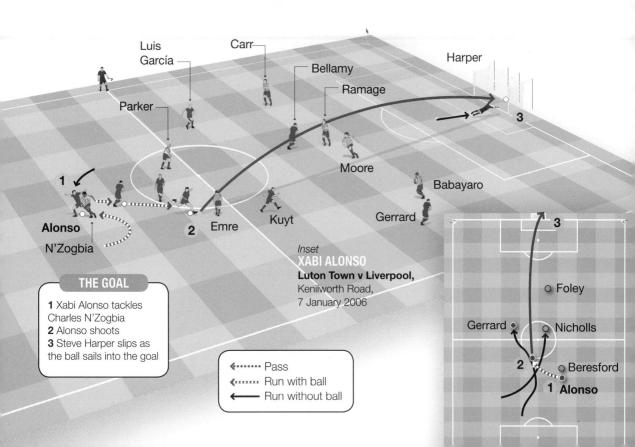

Luis
García

Carr

Bellamy

Ramage

Harper

Parker

Alonso

1

N'Zogbia

2

Emre

Kuyt

Moore

Gerrard

Babayaro

3

Inset
XABI ALONSO
Luton Town v Liverpool,
Kenilworth Road,
7 January 2006

THE GOAL

1 Xabi Alonso tackles
Charles N'Zogbia
2 Alonso shoots
3 Steve Harper slips as
the ball sails into the goal

◀······· Pass
◀╍╍╍╍ Run with ball
◀━━━ Run without ball

3

⬤ Foley

Gerrard ⬤

⬤ Nicholls

2

⬤ Beresford

1 Alonso

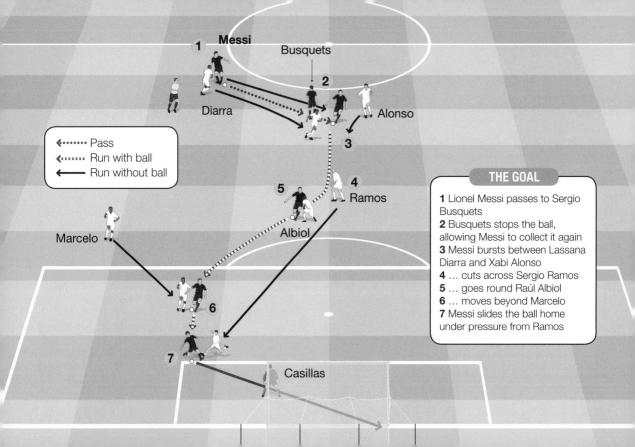

Messi

Busquets

1

2

Diarra

Alonso

3

◄······· Pass
◄······· Run with ball
◄─────── Run without ball

5

4

Ramos

Marcelo

Albiol

6

THE GOAL

1 Lionel Messi passes to Sergio Busquets
2 Busquets stops the ball, allowing Messi to collect it again
3 Messi bursts between Lassana Diarra and Xabi Alonso
4 … cuts across Sergio Ramos
5 … goes round Raúl Albiol
6 … moves beyond Marcelo
7 Messi slides the ball home under pressure from Ramos

7

Casillas

080 LIONEL MESSI
Real Madrid v Barcelona, 27 April 2011
The sizzling solo

Diego Maradona is considered by many to have been the world's greatest footballer. Yet, by the time Lionel Messi had finished with Real Madrid here, many observers were starting to claim that Maradona was not even the best diminutive, left-footed Argentine dribbler who had played for Barcelona.

Messi had left his homeland for the Catalan club at the age of 13 because they offered to pay for treatment of his growth-hormone deficiency while integrating him in their youth system. A decade later that far-sighted decision was reaping huge rewards for the Spanish side almost on a weekly basis. His pair of goals against Madrid took his club tally for the season to 52 and for his Barcelona career as a whole to 179, moving him up to third on their all-time list while still aged only 23.

It was a feat for Messi to rise above the niggly approach adopted by Real during the series of four meetings in 18 days between these teams. Pepe's dismissal for a high foul on the hour meant Barcelona were facing ten men for the fourth consecutive game against their great rivals, while Real coach José Mourinho, the instigator of the spoiling tactics, was also sent to the stands.

From that vantage point Mourinho saw Messi tap home the opening goal and add the late second after weaving his way through five defenders. He would duly be named FIFA's world player of the year for the third time in succession, but now the question had become: "Is he the world's best player of any year?"

THE MATCH

Champions League semi-final, first leg Bernabéu Stadium

Real Madrid 0 Barcelona 2
Messi 76, **Messi 87**
Att: 71,567

"He has a wonderful ability to take players on. We are lucky to have him" **Pep Guardiola, Barcelona coach**

081 SEBASTIAN LARSSON
Tottenham Hotspur v Birmingham City,
2 December 2007 The top-corner outswinger

In the first decade of the new millennium two categories of manager became prominent in English football: firstly those who had learned their trade as players under Sir Alex Ferguson, and secondly those, like the great man himself, who were Glaswegian. As someone who fitted the bill on both counts Alex McLeish seemed a natural choice by Birmingham City when they brought him to the Premier League in 2007.

As a player and manager McLeish had been involved in well over 1,000 games in Scottish football but this match was his first for a club south of the border. He found his feet quickly, enjoying an unexpected win through a spectacular goal by a player he had recalled to the starting line-up.

Sebastian Larsson is renowned for scoring from free kicks but here he demonstrated long-distance accuracy with a moving ball. The Swede tackled Dimitar Berbatov as the Tottenham striker tried to break forward and instantly sent an outswinging effort into the top right-hand corner.

Tottenham had dominated the match despite losing Robbie Keane to a 68th-minute red card, and their despair at defeat was deepened by the fact that a former Arsenal player scored the winning goal. Birmingham's 3–2 victory continued a year of wild excitement at White Hart Lane – Tottenham's 29 fixtures there in 2007 brought an extraordinary average of 4.2 goals per game. Few of those strikes were more dramatic than Larsson's or more memorable for their manager.

"I was a bit tired and thought 'why not have a go'?"
Sebastian Larsson

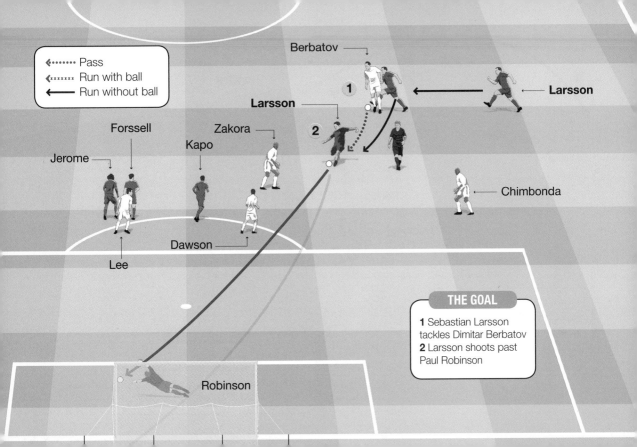

Pass
Run with ball
Run without ball

Berbatov

Larsson

Larsson

1

2

Forssell

Zakora

Kapo

Jerome

Chimbonda

Dawson

Lee

Robinson

THE GOAL

1 Sebastian Larsson
tackles Dimitar Berbatov
2 Larsson shoots past
Paul Robinson

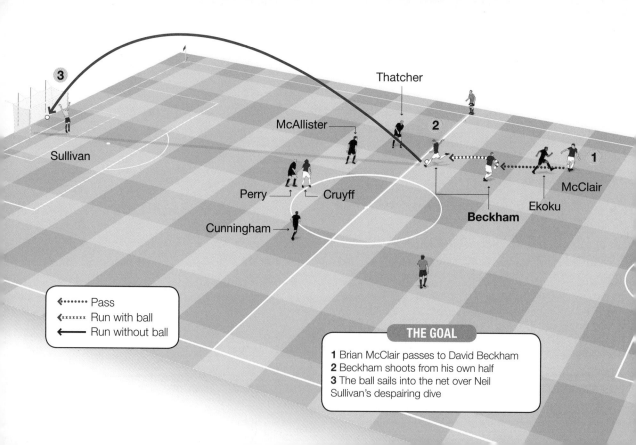

(3)

Thatcher

McAllister

2

Sullivan

Perry → ┌ └ ← Cruyff

Beckham

Ekoku

McClair

1

Cunningham →

◄······· Pass
◄······· Run with ball
◄─── Run without ball

THE GOAL

1 Brian McClair passes to David Beckham
2 Beckham shoots from his own half
3 The ball sails into the net over Neil
Sullivan's despairing dive

082 DAVID BECKHAM
Wimbledon v Manchester United, 17 August 1996
The halfway hit

In the 1996 Charity Shield at Wembley, David Beckham scored from 30 yards against Newcastle United after running clear of the defence and chipping a hopelessly stranded goalkeeper with a shot that bounced before entering the goal. Seven days later, on the other side of London, the Manchester United player outdid himself by scoring against Wimbledon from double the distance and, in contrast, with only a tiny amount of space behind the goalkeeper.

The midfielder was the centre of attention even before his magnificent goal. A regular for United in the previous season, he was now 21 and pushing for a first England call-up. The opening league game of the campaign came as Glenn Hoddle was about to announce his first squad since replacing Terry Venables as manager of the national side.

Beckham had already proved himself the game's outstanding player at Selhurst Park, helping to create United's first two goals, when he collected a pass from Brian McClair in the last minute. His shot carried the ball from inches inside his own half to inches underneath the crossbar and into the net, squeezing over the head of Wimbledon goalkeeper Neil Sullivan.

While United's performance suggested they could retain their title, a target that they duly achieved, Beckham showed he was more than ready for the step up from club football. He made his England debut a fortnight later and he was no flash in the pan, going on to win more than 100 caps: a long international career launched by a long shot.

THE MATCH

**English league
Selhurst Park**

**Wimbledon 0
Manchester United 3**
Cantona 25, Irwin 58,
Beckham 90
Att: 25,786

"For most players it is a dream to do such a thing. It was an incredible goal" Manchester United forward Jordi Cruyff

083 RONNIE WHELAN
Ireland v USSR, 15 June 1988
The giant throw

THE MATCH

**European championship group game
Niedersachsenstadion**

Ireland 1
Whelan 38
USSR 1
Protasov 74
Att: 38,308

Ireland's midfield included Ronnie Whelan, Ray Houghton and Kevin Sheedy, players who had won the English league title during the previous two seasons (the first two with Liverpool, Sheedy with Everton) and who were capable of clever, quick-passing moves. But their country had reached the 1988 European championship in West Germany – their first major tournament – with a direct style of play, and Jack Charlton, the manager, was not about to change his rudimentary methods.

Usually this meant the defence or goalkeeper playing long balls forward over the heads of the midfielders. Against the USSR in Hanover, though, it was an enormous throw-in that brought reward. As Ireland manager many years later Mick McCarthy would pick Rory Delap, famous for his throw-ins, but on this occasion it was McCarthy himself who delivered the long throw, albeit one that travelled in a big arc rather than in the manner of Delap's arrows.

McCarthy hurled the ball so far – beyond the penalty spot – that it caught out the USSR defence, allowing Whelan to shoot without any great challenge from an opponent. The midfielder made such a perfect body shape when shooting – leaping and twisting his body to execute a volley – that the ball flew into the top corner of the net even though it struck him on the shin.

Later in the game another long throw by McCarthy also brought a shot by Whelan, though this was saved by Rinat Dasayev, the goalkeeper. One such remarkable goal was enough for one day.

"A goal to grace any footballing occasion"
TV commentator George Hamilton

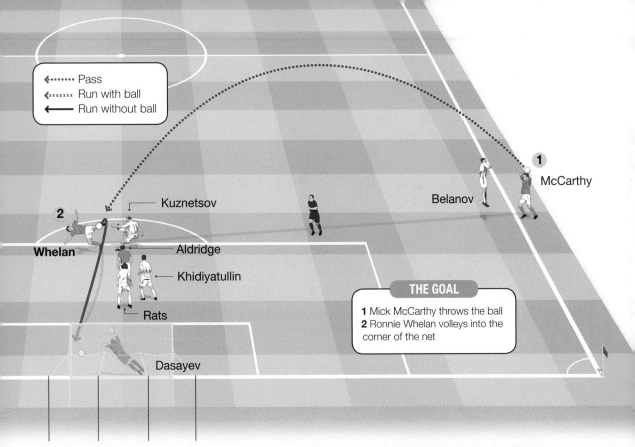

Pass
Run with ball
Run without ball

McCarthy

Belanov

Kuznetsov

2
Whelan

Aldridge

Khidiyatullin

Rats

THE GOAL

1 Mick McCarthy throws the ball
2 Ronnie Whelan volleys into the corner of the net

Dasayev

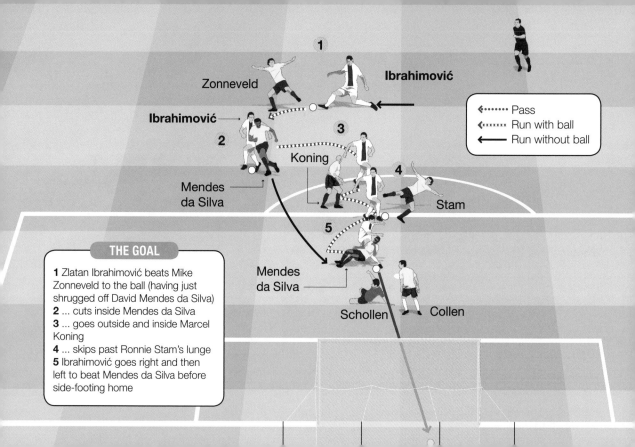

Zonneveld

Ibrahimović

1

Ibrahimović →

2

Koning

3

4

Stam

Mendes
da Silva

5

Mendes
da Silva →

Schollen

Collen

Pass ←·······
Run with ball ←:::::::
Run without ball ←——

THE GOAL

1 Zlatan Ibrahimović beats Mike
Zonneveld to the ball (having just
shrugged off David Mendes da Silva)
2 ... cuts inside Mendes da Silva
3 ... goes outside and inside Marcel
Koning
4 ... skips past Ronnie Stam's lunge
5 Ibrahimović goes right and then
left to beat Mendes da Silva before
side-footing home

084 ZLATAN IBRAHIMOVIĆ
Ajax v NAC Breda, 22 August 2004
The mazy dribble

When Zlatan Ibrahimović helped AC Milan become Italian champions in 2011 it was, incredibly, his eighth domestic league title in a row, spread over spells with five clubs. The first came with Ajax, the next two at Juventus (albeit they were stripped of them for influencing referee appointments), then three at Inter Milan and one at Barcelona.

But the Swede leaves in his wake a trail of chaos as well as trophies. A former headmistress considered him "one of the most unruly pupils we have ever had". Recalling dressing-room spats, the player admitted: "I was a savage, a lunatic, and I couldn't control my temper."

The background to this goal was classic Ibrahimović. Playing for Sweden four days earlier, his tackle injured Rafael van der Vaart, the Holland striker and his Ajax team-mate, who claimed the Swede had hurt him deliberately (his colleague denied that, though Ibrahimović did confess later that on another occasion he threatened to break his legs). Ajax fans, sympathetic to van der Vaart, booed Ibrahimović when he took the field against NAC Breda. What might have broken mentally weaker players did not faze Ibrahimović.

In a seemingly endless dribble he beat or held off David Mendes da Silva four times, Marcel Koning twice and two other players once each before scoring. The injured van der Vaart looked on stony-faced. Days later the Swede was sold to Juventus after refusing to play alongside his team-mate. Inevitably, his Ajax career had ended in tears and triumph.

THE MATCH

Dutch league
Amsterdam Arena

Ajax 6
Ibrahimović 13,
Zonneveld og 41,
Heitinga 51, Sneijder 70,
Ibrahimović 76, Maxwell 86
NAC Breda 2
Cornelisse 11, Slot 82
Att: 46,124

"I searched for a moment to shoot. It did not come so I kept on going past different players" **Zlatan Ibrahimović**

085 DAVID GINOLA
Barnsley v Tottenham Hotspur, 16 March 1999
The crisscross trail

A penchant for star names over effective team players has characterised Tottenham Hotspur, who went half a century without a league title after achieving the league and FA Cup double in 1960–61. In that barren spell seven different players from the club won one of the annual awards voted for by journalists and players, compared with only five from Arsenal, who were champions six times during that period.

But in 1999 Tottenham were guided by George Graham, who was known for his mistrust of flamboyant players. On arriving as manager he warned David Ginola, the skilful winger, to follow his game plan – rather than play off the cuff – or leave. The Frenchman did as he was told, and, when the manager demanded more goals, he supplied those as well, most memorably against Barnsley. As ever Spurs would get nowhere near the title but journalists and players alike voted Ginola the best player of the 1998–99 season.

Ginola's run lit up a tedious game. Starting on the left, he cut inside Nicky Eaden, knocked the ball past a diving Clayton Blackmore, moved the other way to escape from Robin van der Laan, swayed inside Arjan de Zeeuw and sidefooted past Tony Bullock. Graham's response? Very good, but he would save full praise for when the Frenchman scored a few tap-ins.

Graham had been an unpopular appointment as a former player and manager with big rivals Arsenal and for his fondness of defensive football. But late in this match Tottenham fans chanted Graham's name for the first time since he became manager five months earlier. Such was the power of Ginola's goal.

"It was an unbelievable goal" **Barnsley defender Chris Morgan**

THE MATCH

**FA Cup sixth round
Oakwell**

**Barnsley 0
Tottenham Hotspur 1**
Ginola 68
Att: 18,793

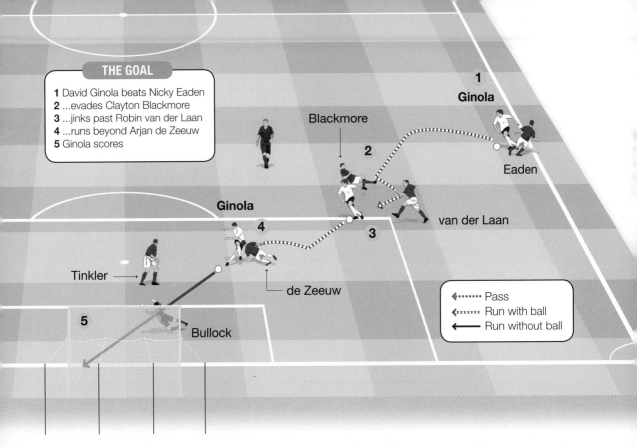

THE GOAL

1 David Ginola beats Nicky Eaden
2 ...evades Clayton Blackmore
3 ...jinks past Robin van der Laan
4 ...runs beyond Arjan de Zeeuw
5 Ginola scores

1
Ginola

Eaden

Blackmore
2

Ginola
4

3

van der Laan

Tinkler →

de Zeeuw

5

Bullock

◄······· Pass
◄▪▪▪▪▪▪▪ Run with ball
◄━━━━━ Run without ball

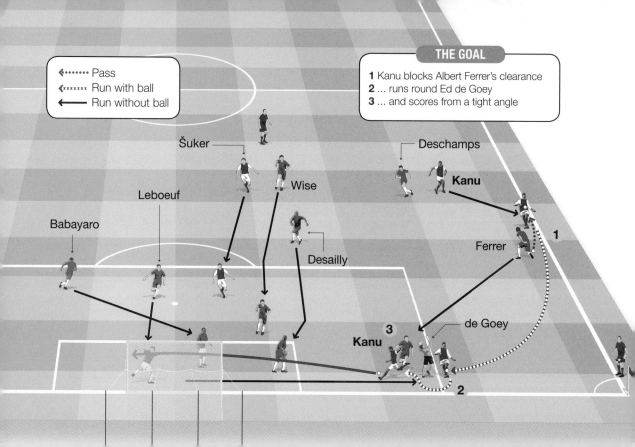

Pass ←·······

Run with ball ←:::::::

Run without ball ←——

THE GOAL

1 Kanu blocks Albert Ferrer's clearance
2 ... runs round Ed de Goey
3 ... and scores from a tight angle

Šuker

Deschamps

Kanu

Wise

Leboeuf

Babayaro

Desailly

Ferrer

de Goey

3
Kanu

1

2

086 KANU

Chelsea v Arsenal, 23 October 1999
The precision in the puddles

THE MATCH

**English league
Stamford Bridge**

Chelsea 2
Flo 38, Petrescu 52
Arsenal 3
Kanu 75, Kanu 83,
Kanu 90+2
Att: 34,958

Kanu's perfect balance was always a striking attribute and he never used it to better effect than when staying upright while splashing through the Stamford Bridge puddles in this game. A pitch that was initially perfect quickly became waterlogged when heavy rain began falling during the second half, to the liking of the Nigerian, who showed why he would be named African Footballer of the Year for 1999.

Deep into the final quarter of the match, Chelsea had still to concede their first home league goal of the season. They had beaten both Manchester United and Galatasaray 5–0 earlier in the month and they led 2–0 here. Step forward Kanu. First he prodded the ball past Chelsea goalkeeper Ed de Goey, causing a spray as he did so, then he collected a cross by Marc Overmars, turned and smashed home the equaliser.

Two minutes into stoppage time Arsenal's comeback – and Kanu's hat-trick – were completed in extraordinary fashion. The forward charged down an attempted clearance by Chelsea right-back Albert Ferrer and reached the left-hand byline where he dribbled round de Goey, who had left his penalty area. Marcel Desailly and Frank Leboeuf still blocked his path to goal but, from an acute angle, he simply lifted his shot over the two centre-backs into the far corner of the net.

Pre-match expectations of roughness were met with eight players booked (four from each side). But Kanu was not among them as he produced an act of beauty among the beasts.

"I was never going to cross. Immediately I beat the keeper my mind was on how to score" Kanu

087 PELÉ
Brazil v Mexico, 30 May 1962
The balletic bulldozer

He was only 21, but Pelé was already considered to be the world's best player. The centre forward had helped Brazil to their World Cup triumph four years earlier – scoring a hat-trick in the semi-final against France and two more in the win over Sweden in the final – and here he inspired them as they began the defence of their crown in Chile.

Brazil had also opened their World Cup campaigns of 1950 and 1954 against Mexico, recording wins of 4–0 and 5–0, but this time the fixture proved a far tougher assignment. In fact the Mexicans wasted several good scoring opportunities themselves before Pelé finally engineered a breakthrough for Brazil 11 minutes into the second half, evading challenges to cross for Mario Zagallo to head home.

Then came Pelé's masterpiece. Starting on the right touchline he hit the ball one side of Pedro Nájera while running round the other, outsprinted Salvador Reyes, crashed through the tackle of José Villegas, shrugged off Raúl Cárdenas and drilled home an unstoppable shot. His great skill on the ball means the kind of ruggedness in 50–50 contests that he showed here is often overlooked. At the 1970 World Cup, recalled for its beauty, he committed twice as many fouls as any team-mate.

Sadly for Pelé, he suffered a groin injury early in the next game against Czechoslovakia and his tournament was over. But Brazil went on to retain the trophy, so he could point to his remarkable goal as having contributed to their success.

THE MATCH

**World Cup group game
Estadio Sausalito**

Brazil 2
Zagallo 56, **Pelé 73**
Mexico 0
Att: 10,484

"Pelé showed the form that has won him the reputation of being the world's greatest footballer" Reuters

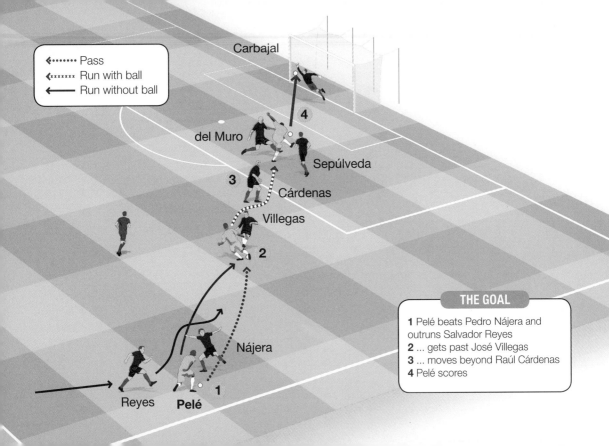

Carbajal

del Muro

Sepúlveda

Cárdenas

Villegas

Nájera

Reyes   **Pelé**

THE GOAL

1 Pelé beats Pedro Nájera and outruns Salvador Reyes
2 ... gets past José Villegas
3 ... moves beyond Raúl Cárdenas
4 Pelé scores

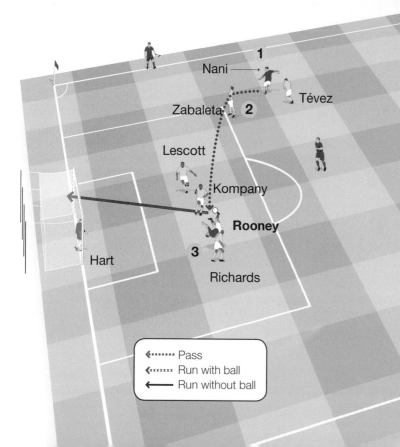

Nani →

1

Tévez

Zabaleta   2

Lescott

Kompany

Rooney

3

Hart

Richards

THE GOAL

1 Nani crosses the ball
2 It deflects off Pablo
Zabaleta
3 Wayne Rooney volleys
it into the net

◄······· Pass
◄······· Run with ball
◄——— Run without ball

088 WAYNE ROONEY
Manchester United v Manchester City,
12 February 2011 The aerobatic display

Manchester United's signing of Wayne Rooney in 2004 had proved highly successful for both parties, but club and player had cause for concern when Manchester City visited Old Trafford for this match. The takeover of City by a member of the Abu Dhabi royal family was funding their challenge to United's position as the leading English club of the 21st century, while Rooney himself had endured troubled times.

The striker had played poorly for most of 2010, with United manager Sir Alex Ferguson blaming media scrutiny of his private life. Late in the year Rooney even asked to leave the club, claiming they were not ambitious, but, with City ready to sign him, he did a U-turn and agreed to stay at Old Trafford.

Rooney had regained some form by the time he faced City but, with 12 minutes of the derby left, he had contributed little as a 1–1 draw loomed. However when Nani's deflected cross fell just behind him in the penalty area he turned his back on the City goal, leapt high and sent a thunderous overhead volley into the far corner of the net.

It was, the player said, his first such overhead strike since his school days and, as he celebrated wildly, it was as if the goal had brought an official end to his unhappy spell. It also clinched a victory that took United eight points clear of their local rivals en route to yet another league title. For the time being City's advance had been repelled.

"When he was up there I was thinking, 'What's he doing?' And then when it went in the net I was speechless for about five seconds"
Manchester City defender Micah Richards

089 NAYIM
Real Zaragoza v Arsenal, 10 May 1995
The touchline lob

Five years spent across North London at Tottenham Hotspur meant Nayim was already familiar to Arsenal. But the Spanish midfielder left his name indelibly in Arsenal minds when he scored a goal for Real Zaragoza that combined two separate elements that would stand alone as unforgettable – a 40-yard lob from near the touchline and a last-minute winning goal in a cup final.

Zaragoza had already notched up one London victim with their semi-final win over Chelsea, but Arsenal were favourites to become the first club to retain the Cup Winners' Cup, having beaten Parma in the final 12 months earlier. It would be the perfect way for Stewart Houston to round off his three-month spell as their caretaker manager.

Arsenal had won their semi-final against Sampdoria in a penalty shoot-out in which David Seaman saved three spot kicks, but, with another shoot-out looming in the final, the goalkeeper turned from hero to villain. Fourteen seconds of extra-time remained when Nayim spotted he had strayed off his line: his shot rose high into the Paris sky and fell just under the crossbar, helped over the line by Seaman's flailing hand.

Later in his career Seaman was given two reminders of the incident. In 2002 Ronaldinho chipped him from a similar place for Brazil's winning goal against England in the World Cup quarter-finals. Two years earlier, in what was Arsenal's next European final, they lost in the UEFA Cup to Galatasaray in a penalty shoot-out. The winning kick was struck by Gheorghe Popescu, once of … Tottenham.

"As soon as he hit it I knew I was in trouble. It was a superb strike" Arsenal goalkeeper David Seaman

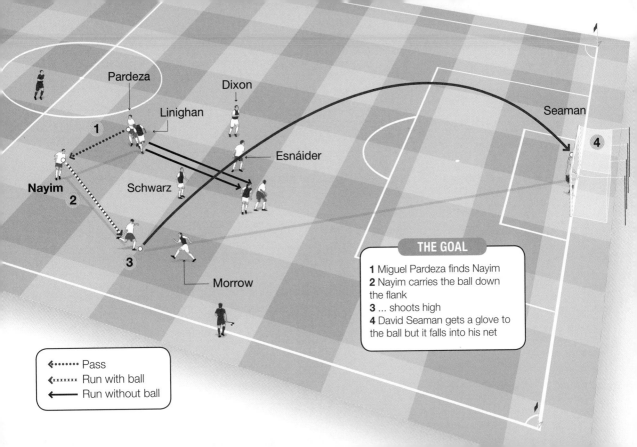

Pardeza

Dixon

Linighan

Seaman

Esnáider

1

Nayim

2

Schwarz

3

Morrow

THE GOAL

1 Miguel Pardeza finds Nayim
2 Nayim carries the ball down the flank
3 ... shoots high
4 David Seaman gets a glove to the ball but it falls into his net

4

◀······· Pass
◀····· Run with ball
◀─── Run without ball

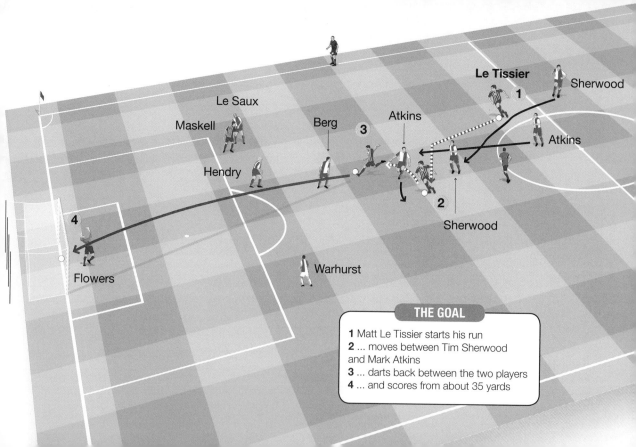

Le Tissier

Sherwood

Le Saux

Maskell

Berg

3

Atkins

Atkins

Hendry

2

Sherwood

4

Flowers

Warhurst

THE GOAL

1 Matt Le Tissier starts his run

2 ... moves between Tim Sherwood and Mark Atkins

3 ... darts back between the two players

4 ... and scores from about 35 yards

090 MATT LE TISSIER
Blackburn Rovers v Southampton, 10 December 1994
The slalom

Admittedly this goal by Matt Le Tissier left his Southampton team still trailing 3–2 with only 12 minutes left, but anyone else in his position might have displayed at least a modicum of joy after producing such an extraordinary piece of skill. But the player simply walked back to his own half for the restart while urging his team-mates to collect the ball from the net.

Such nonchalance, so characteristic of Le Tissier, was sometimes mistaken for laziness. That, in turn, was thought to tie in with his apparent lack of ambition. Talented enough to have forced a move to a leading club if he desired, he preferred instead to stay in familiar surroundings and fight almost perennial relegation battles with Southampton.

This defeat against Blackburn, the Premier League leaders, left Southampton only three points clear of the drop zone, but Le Tissier, single-handedly, almost earned a draw. His shot in the closing minutes would have completed his hat-trick, but it was saved by the feet of Tim Flowers, his good friend and a former Southampton goalkeeper.

So Southampton supporters had to find consolation in their memories of his incredible second goal. Collecting a pass just to the right of the centre circle, Le Tissier swerved inside and out to evade the attentions of Mark Atkins and Tim Sherwood, the Blackburn midfielders, before steering the ball beyond Flowers from 35 yards. Football followers around the country marvelled at the goal, even if it was all in a day's work for the goalscorer.

"It was a wonderful goal – it will probably win goal of the season [it did indeed]" **Blackburn manager Kenny Dalglish**

091 DEJAN SAVIĆEVIĆ
AC Milan v Barcelona, 18 May 1994
The angled chip

Disharmony was inevitable when AC Milan stock-piled six high-profile foreign players in the early 1990s, despite quotas restricting them to using only three in Italian league and European games. Dejan Savićević, who helped Red Star Belgrade win the European Cup in 1991, a year before his move to Italy, was among the unlucky ones, spending much of his first 18 months at the club sitting in the stands.

The Montenegrin wanted to leave Milan but was persuaded to stay by Silvio Berlusconi, the club's president, who called him "The Genius". Barcelona discovered the accuracy of that nickname when the attacking midfielder tormented them in this match, having finally established himself in the team in recent months.

The match featured Europe's strongest pair by a distance. Milan had just won their third successive domestic league title and Barcelona their fourth, but their strategies differed. That season the Spanish team's entertaining approach under Johan Cruyff brought 91 league goals to only 36 by Fabio Capello's dour Italian side. Cruyff implied beforehand that a Milan victory in Athens would set a trend for defensive football.

Yet it was Milan who produced an irresistible, attacking display, with Savićević to the fore. They were already leading 2–0 when he charged down an attempted clearance by Miguel Nadal and sent an audacious lob over Andoni Zubizarreta, the back-pedalling goalkeeper. At that moment, all his time sidelined by the foreigner-restriction rule seemed a terrible waste.

"It's my gift to our president [Milan owner Silvio Berlusconi]"
Dejan Savićević

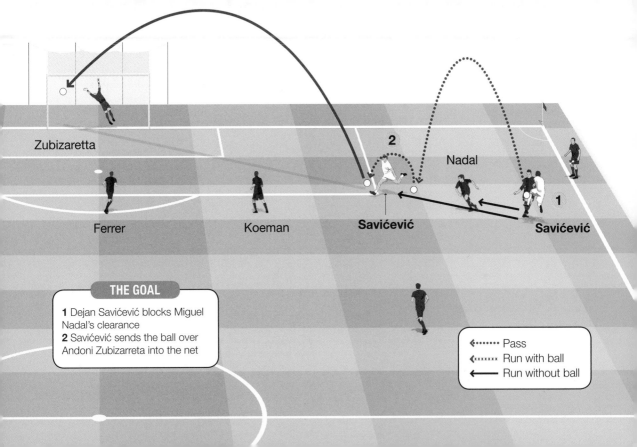

Zubizaretta

Ferrer

Koeman

Savićević

2

Nadal

Savićević

1

THE GOAL

1 Dejan Savićević blocks Miguel Nadal's clearance
2 Savićević sends the ball over Andoni Zubizarreta into the net

◄······ Pass
◄······ Run with ball
◄—— Run without ball

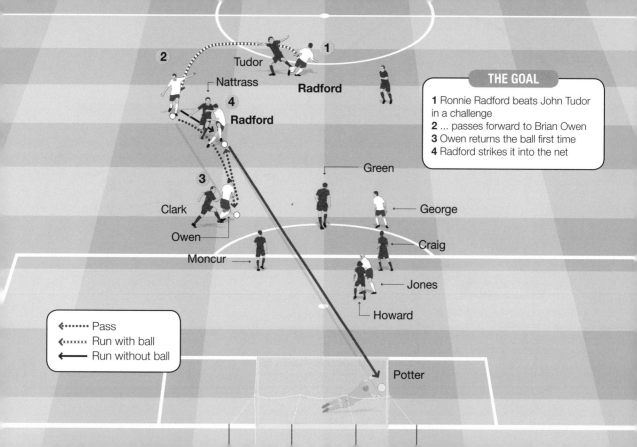

Tudor

Radford

THE GOAL

1 Ronnie Radford beats John Tudor in a challenge
2 ... passes forward to Brian Owen
3 Owen returns the ball first time
4 Radford strikes it into the net

Nattrass

Radford

Green

Clark

George

Owen

Craig

Moncur

Jones

Howard

.... Pass
.... Run with ball
⟵ Run without ball

Potter

092 RONNIE RADFORD

Hereford United v Newcastle United, 5 February 1972
The blast among the bobbles

When the Midland Electricity Board said they could not guarantee full power during this match the kick-off was moved forward half an hour to 2.30 pm. But the floodlights at Hereford United's Edgar Street did serve one purpose – many spectators climbed them to get a better view in a small ground packed to capacity.

The prospect of an FA Cup match between a top-flight and non-league team was relished, all the more so after five postponements because of wintry weather, two for the original game in Newcastle, which ended 2–2, and three for the replay. More than 60 reporters attended instead of the usual four for Southern League games. Newcastle United's players endured frustration, though. Stuck in a hotel in nearby Worcester as the replay kept being delayed, they had to send for more clothes from home.

Hereford had just fallen behind when, with four minutes left, Ronnie Radford, a joiner by trade, won a 50–50 challenge with John Tudor in midfield. The Hereford player scrambled to his feet, played a one-two with Brian Owen and, with the ball bobbling in the hard, thick mud, smashed it home from long distance.

Fans swamped the goalscorer, and they returned to the pitch twice more – after Ricky George's extra-time winner and the final whistle. A few months later Hereford's chances of achieving more non-league heroics were over: they were voted into the league, their case strengthened by that result and Radford's extraordinary goal.

> "I'll never know how he dragged from his boots the strength to fire that shot" **Hereford player-manager Colin Addison**

THE MATCH

FA Cup
fourth round replay
Edgar Street

Hereford United 2
Radford 86, George 103
Newcastle United 1
Macdonald 82
Att: 15,500

093 MARIO STANIĆ
Chelsea v West Ham United, 19 August 2000
The juggle on the move

When Chelsea decided to sign Mario Stanić from Italian club Parma in the summer of 2000, perhaps they were encouraged by how Gianfranco Zola had made the same move so successfully four years earlier. If becoming another Zola was an almost impossible task, though, Stanić did at least set about emulating Gus Poyet during a league debut which could hardly have gone better.

Just as happened the previous season, Chelsea lit up Stamford Bridge on the opening day of the league campaign with four goals that included a spectacular right-footed volley from a midfielder bursting forward late in the game. For Poyet 12 months earlier, read Stanić here. For good measure, these goals came at the same end of the ground, and the pair also found the net with a header elsewhere in the match.

Stanić, who had helped Croatia reach the World Cup semi-finals in 1998, controlled the ball as he turned towards goal about 40 yards out. Then he kept it up with his thigh and foot before, still without it having touched the ground, he volleyed a shot that flew into the roof of the net.

Sadly for Stanić, he injured his knee in his next Chelsea appearance and when he returned five months later the manager who had signed him, Gianluca Vialli, had been sacked. The Croatian was never able to establish himself fully under Claudio Ranieri, Vialli's successor. Injuries played a part, but a total of only 39 league starts in four seasons at the club was a big disappointment for a player who had begun so remarkably.

"I was screaming at him to pass the ball and then he did that. Sheer brilliance" **Chelsea forward Jimmy Floyd Hasselbaink**

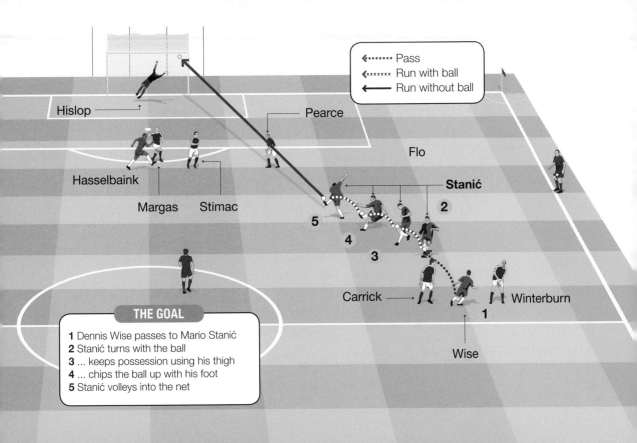

Pass
Run with ball
Run without ball

Hislop

Pearce

Flo

Hasselbaink

Stanić

Margas   Stimac

2

5

4

3

Carrick

1

Winterburn

Wise

THE GOAL

1 Dennis Wise passes to Mario Stanić
2 Stanić turns with the ball
3 ... keeps possession using his thigh
4 ... chips the ball up with his foot
5 Stanić volleys into the net

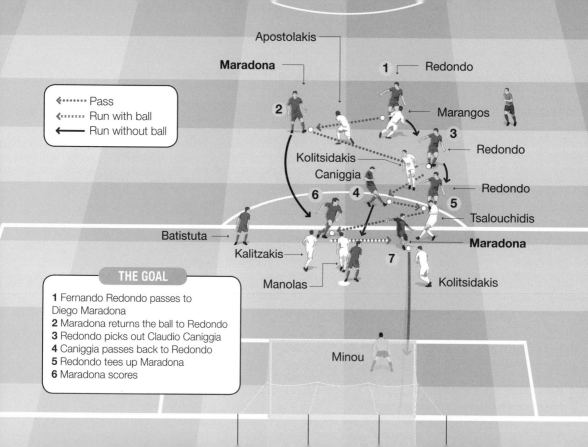

Apostolakis

Maradona

1 Redondo

Marangos

Pass

Run with ball

Run without ball

2

3

Redondo

Kolitsidakis

Redondo

Caniggia

6 **4** **5**

Tsalouchidis

Batistuta

Maradona

Kalitzakis

7

Manolas

Kolitsidakis

THE GOAL

1 Fernando Redondo passes to
Diego Maradona
2 Maradona returns the ball to Redondo
3 Redondo picks out Claudio Caniggia
4 Caniggia passes back to Redondo
5 Redondo tees up Maradona
6 Maradona scores

Minou

094 DIEGO MARADONA
Argentina v Greece, 21 June 1994
The pinball passing move

At the 1982 World Cup Diego Maradona was sent off for Argentina against Brazil, in 1986 he inspired his country to become world champions and, four years later, he was left in tears by a defeat to West Germany in the final. The little master had played a central role in three successive World Cups and he extended that sequence to four in 1994, a tournament he began with ingenuity and ended in infamy.

The memory of a 5–0 home defeat by Colombia the previous autumn was still fresh for Argentina as they opened their campaign in the United States, but a comfortable victory over Greece gave them confidence. Furthermore, their third goal encouraged the belief that they might reach a third consecutive final, guided there by Maradona.

The build-up was so bewilderingly fast that a slow-motion replay must be viewed to comprehend it properly. Fernando Redondo executed a rapid one-two with Maradona and then exchanged passes even quicker with Claudio Caniggia as Greek opponents were sent up blind alleys. Caniggia then found Maradona with another first-time pass, and the latter created space for a shot that flew into the corner of the net.

But just as Maradona's solo goal against England in 1986 came shortly after his hand-ball goal, this effort was also tainted. He played the next match against Nigeria but was found to have taken banned substances that increased concentration and physical ability. His was kicked out of the tournament and his eventful World Cup career was over.

"Maradona evoked glories of old"
Journalist and author Brian Glanville

THE MATCH

**World Cup group game
Foxboro Stadium USA**

Argentina 4
Batistuta 2, Batistuta 45,
Maradona 60,
Batistuta pen. 89
Greece 0
Att: 53,486

095 STEVEN REID
Wigan Athletic v Blackburn Rovers,
31 December 2005 The bullet

Steven Reid spent large parts of his seven-year stint at Blackburn Rovers sidelined by injury. He was out for three months in his first season there, 2003–04, and suffered absences of 14 months from September 2006 and 11 months from September 2008. Conversely, he might have inflicted injury on another player if anyone had been brave or quick enough to move into the path of his thunderous shot against Wigan Athletic.

The Ireland international's long-legged athleticism marked him out whether playing at right back or – his more frequent position at Blackburn – in midfield. When Wigan defender Pascal Chimbonda headed clear from David Bentley's right-wing cross, Reid was onto the loose ball in a flash, striding forward and sending it into the goal in a blur from 25 yards out. The ball would have

continued to rise much higher had it not struck the roof of the net.

If Reid's first goal for nine months was a novelty, so was the fixture itself – the first league meeting between these two North West clubs whose stadiums are just 25 miles apart. Wigan's promotion the previous summer had concluded their nine-year march from the league's bottom division to the top flight, and their progress continued as they sat in fifth place before this match.

Reid's strike helped Blackburn towards an impressive victory that he was clearly anxious to secure: 20 minutes from the end of the game he was booked for time-wasting. How Wigan must have wished he had shown a similar lack of urgency earlier in the game.

"A remarkable goal"
Blackburn manager Mark Hughes

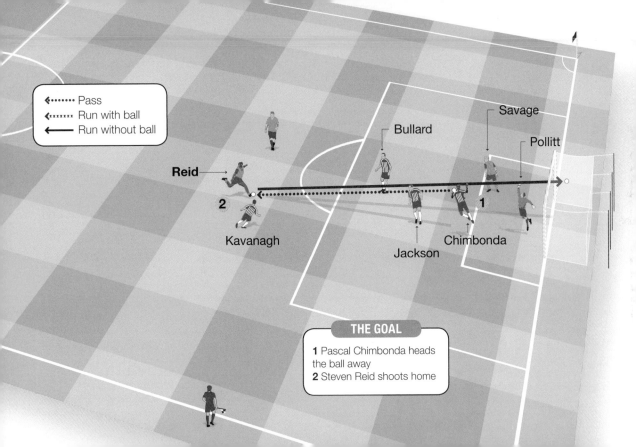

Pass
Run with ball
Run without ball

Reid

Bullard

Savage

Pollitt

2

Kavanagh

Jackson

Chimbonda

1

THE GOAL

1 Pascal Chimbonda heads
the ball away
2 Steven Reid shoots home

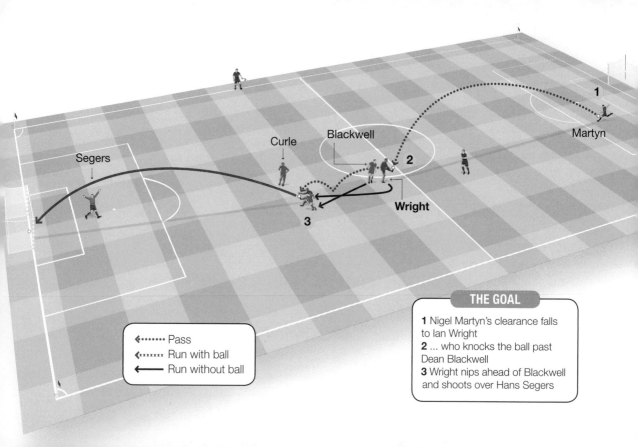

Segers

Curle

Blackwell

Martyn

Wright

1

2

3

······▶ Pass

······▶ Run with ball

———▶ Run without ball

THE GOAL

1 Nigel Martyn's clearance falls to Ian Wright

2 ... who knocks the ball past Dean Blackwell

3 Wright nips ahead of Blackwell and shoots over Hans Segers

096 IAN WRIGHT
Wimbledon v Crystal Palace, 4 May 1991
The direct line

"Ian Wright, Wright, Wright" went the terrace chant, and it summed up the scoring in this game. The popular Crystal Palace striker's hat-trick constituted the only goals of a match that all but confirmed his team's eventual finishing position of third in the top flight, ten places higher than the previous best in their history.

For a club promoted only two years beforehand it had been a steep rise, matching that of the player himself, who was plucked from the non-leagues by Palace at 21 and now, six years later, had recently made his England debut. Arsenal, the champions, completed his climb to the top of the club ladder by signing him early the next season.

This was Wimbledon's final home game at Plough Lane, their now-dilapidated home of 79 years, and they were put in their place by the team who would be their landlords at Selhurst Park from the following season. Wimbledon were themselves punching above their weight as they headed for a final position of seventh, but they were knocked to the canvas here, notably by the blow of Wright's stunning second goal.

When a clearance by Palace goalkeeper Nigel Martyn found him on the edge of the centre circle, Wright flicked the ball past Dean Blackwell, the last defender, and, despite having the chance to carry it towards the penalty area unhindered, simply smashed a lob over Hans Segers into the net from about 40 yards. Having started his professional career late, Wright was a man in a hurry.

"He's intuitive and instinctive. If you make him think, the intuition is lost" Crystal Palace manager Steve Coppell

---

THE MATCH

English league
Plough Lane

Wimbledon 0
Crystal Palace 3
Wright 54, **Wright 60**,
Wright 72
Att: 10,002

097 RICKY VILLA
Tottenham Hotspur v Manchester City, 14 May 1981
The weaving path

Tottenham Hotspur fans clung to omens ahead of the FA Cup final. The team had won at least one trophy in each of 1901, 1921, 1951, 1961 and 1971, so why not 1981? Furthermore, in China it was the year of the cockerel, and the club's emblem was a cockerel standing on a football.

A more concrete reason for predicting victory over Manchester City was the presence of Ossie Ardiles and Ricky Villa, World Cup winning midfielders with Argentina in 1978 and the first South Americans to appear in an FA Cup final for 29 years. Yet Villa struggled in the first match, a 1–1 draw, and was substituted, a decision that upset him deeply and seemed to reinforce his desire to leave the club.

But five days later, in only the second FA Cup final replay since 1912 and the first held at Wembley, Villa gave Tottenham an early lead, only for Steve MacKenzie, City's 19-year-old, to equalise quickly with a thunderous volley. It had progressed to 2–2 with 15 minutes left and the scene was set for the extraordinary winner.

The bearded Villa carried the ball to the edge of the penalty area, cut inside Tommy Caton and Ray Ranson and then swayed across the retreating Caton before poking a shot past Joe Corrigan, the advancing goalkeeper. Afterwards the Argentine said he might change his mind and stay in England – he did indeed, playing for Tottenham for two more years. That decision was doubtless encouraged by the fans' chant at the final whistle of: "Argentina, Argentina".

"There will never be another goal like Ricky Villa's"
Tottenham team-mate Glenn Hoddle

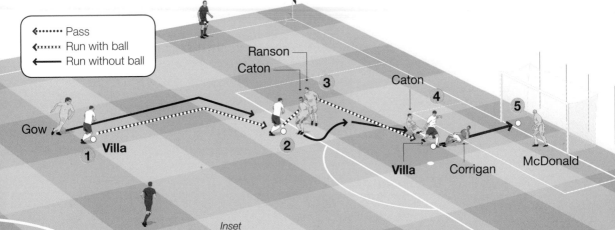

←······ Pass
←······ Run with ball
←—— Run without ball

Ranson
Caton

3

Caton

4

5

Gow

1 **Villa**

2

Villa Corrigan

McDonald

Inset
STEVE MACKENZIE
Tottenham Hotspur v Manchester City

THE GOAL

1 Ricky Villa advances, followed by Gerry Gow
2 Villa cuts inside Tommy Caton
3 ... moves beyond Ray Ranson
4 ... changes direction and dribbles past Caton again
5 Villa scores

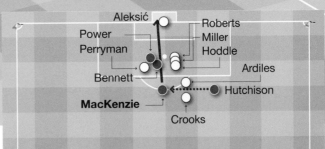

Aleksić

Power
Perryman

Roberts
Miller
Hoddle

Bennett

Ardiles

Hutchison

MacKenzie

Crooks

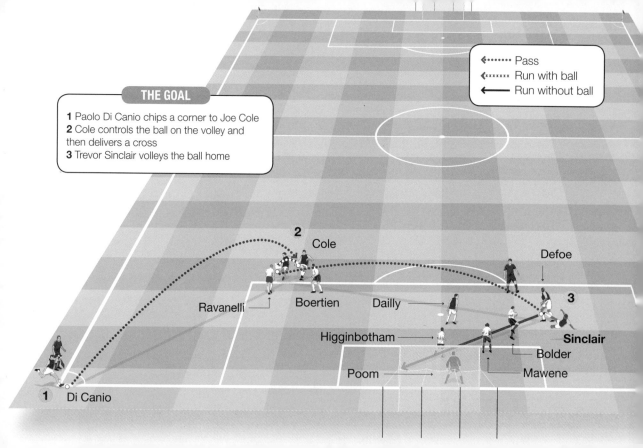

THE GOAL

1 Paolo Di Canio chips a corner to Joe Cole
2 Cole controls the ball on the volley and then delivers a cross
3 Trevor Sinclair volleys the ball home

←······· Pass
←:::::::: Run with ball
←——— Run without ball

2 Cole

Defoe

Ravanelli

Boertien

Dailly

3

Higginbotham

Sinclair

Poom

Bolder

Mawene

1 Di Canio

098 TREVOR SINCLAIR
West Ham United v Derby County, 26 December 2001
The leap and lash

On Boxing Day 2000 Trevor Sinclair scored with a 25-yard volley to help West Ham United beat Charlton Athletic 5–0 at Upton Park. Those home fans present who also turned up at the ground exactly a year later might not have dared hope for something similar. But that is what happened, from another thrashing to another – even more – dramatic goal from Sinclair.

The West Ham team under manager Glenn Roeder certainly adhered to the club's reputation for playing attractive football. Paolo Di Canio, the maverick Italian, was their talisman while Sinclair, Joe Cole, Michael Carrick and Jermain Defoe were a quartet of exciting present or future England players.

Di Canio began the move for Sinclair's goal, impudently chipping the ball from a corner – rather than passing along the ground, as lesser players would have done – so that Joe Cole could control the ball in the air. Cole entered into the spirit, tapping the ball up with his first touch and crossing with his second. At the far post stood Sinclair, who twisted his body in mid-air and smashed a volley into the far corner of the net.

The ball had not touched the floor since the corner was taken, and no doubt Sinclair was finding it hard to keep his feet on the ground having made his England debut against Sweden the previous month at the advanced age of 28. His exciting talent was recognised further the next summer when he started England's final three matches in their run to the World Cup quarter-finals.

"It was a stunning goal. He showed great technique and it was a goal straight out of the coaching manual" West Ham manager Glenn Roeder

099 DENNIS BERGKAMP
Newcastle United v Arsenal, 2 March 2002
The twinkle-toe turn

THE MATCH

**English league
St James' Park**

**Newcastle United 0
Arsenal 2**
Bergkamp 11,
Campbell 41
Att: 52,067

The only reservation about featuring this goal is a concern over whether Dennis Bergkamp actually meant it. In the blink of an eye, the Arsenal forward's flick left him goal side of Nikos Dabizas, his marker, and able to steer the ball into the net. For other players, a fluke might be assumed, but the Dutchman is among a handful of gifted individuals who could be given the benefit of the doubt in such circumstances.

Not that Bergkamp had been enjoying a particularly impressive season. In fact he would probably not even have started this match if Thierry Henry had been fit. The Frenchman was among nine senior Arsenal players unavailable, which encouraged Newcastle United, second in the Premier League, to believe they could extend their one-point advantage over the third-placed visitors.

But such hopes seemed forlorn once Bergkamp had performed his party trick. Collecting Robert Pirès's forward pass with his back to goal, he flicked the ball to his right and spun the other way. To some, it looked as though he meant to run across Dabizas rather than behind him. Whatever the truth, he did the latter and met the ball again before prodding it home. Either way it was a wonderfully balletic moment.

Later in the month Arsenal beat Newcastle again in the FA Cup quarter-finals. Those two victories, with Bergkamp highly influential on both occasions, proved big steps on the path to a league and FA Cup double for Arsène Wenger's team.

"You are blessed when you witness something like that"
Arsenal manager Arsène Wenger

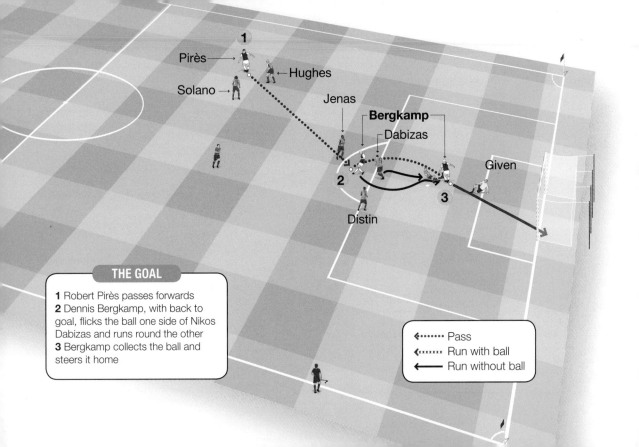

Pirès

Solano

Hughes

Jenas

Bergkamp

Dabizas

Given

Distin

THE GOAL

1 Robert Pirès passes forwards
2 Dennis Bergkamp, with back to goal, flicks the ball one side of Nikos Dabizas and runs round the other
3 Bergkamp collects the ball and steers it home

←······· Pass
←:::::::: Run with ball
←─── Run without ball

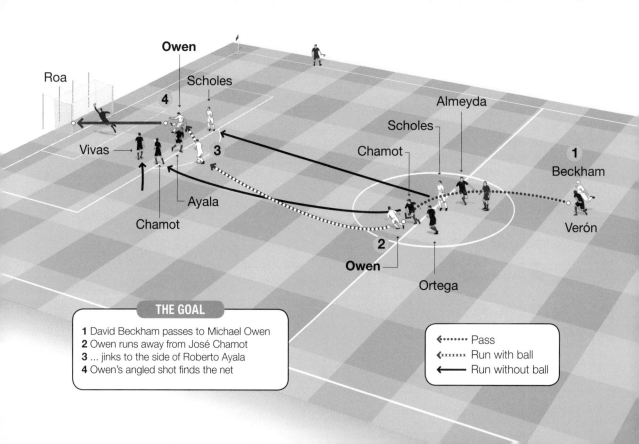

Roa

Vivas →

Chamot

Ayala

Owen

Scholes

4

3

Chamot

Scholes

Almeyda

1

Beckham

2

Owen

Ortega

Verón

THE GOAL

1 David Beckham passes to Michael Owen
2 Owen runs away from José Chamot
3 ... jinks to the side of Roberto Ayala
4 Owen's angled shot finds the net

←······· Pass
←······· Run with ball
←——— Run without ball

100 MICHAEL OWEN
Argentina v England, 30 June 1998
The dash and shimmy

Most of Michael Owen's significant statistics relate to youth. He scored 40 England goals by the age of 27 and won his 89th cap at 28, but neither tally had increased by his 32nd birthday. His debut in February 1998 made him the youngest England player of the century, and three months later he became their youngest goalscorer ever.

Aptly, Owen's greatest England goal came at the tender age of 18. The circumstances alone made it momentous. With 28 million people watching in the UK, his strike put England in front against their big footballing foes just 11 minutes after their opponents had taken an early lead. Thus there was admiration in equal measure both for his brilliance and his poise under pressure.

Owen had not made the starting line-up when England's World Cup campaign in France

began, but his goal as a substitute against Romania persuaded head coach Glenn Hoddle he was ready. This was proved beyond doubt in St Etienne when he tore past José Chamot, left Roberto Ayala flat-footed with a wiggle of his hips and clipped the ball into the top corner.

Argentina's run of eight successive clean sheets had already ended when Owen's running with the ball induced a foul by Ayala that led to England's penalty equaliser. But the speed that caused defences such trouble would be reduced by hamstring injuries, although it didn't stop him turning out subsequently for England, Liverpool, Newcastle United, Real Madrid and Manchester United. But, for many, he will forever be known by his early nickname – The Boy Wonder.

"I will remember it until the day I die"
Michael Owen

THE GOALS

001 **Roberto Carlos**, France v Brazil, 1997
002 **Samir Nasri**, Arsenal v Porto, 2010
003 **Eric Cantona**, Manchester Utd v Sunderland, 1996
004 **Carlos Alberto**, Brazil v Italy, 1970
005 **Michael Essien**, Chelsea v Arsenal, 2006
006 **Peter Beardsley**, Liverpool v Nottingham Forest, 1988
007 **Wesley Sneijder**, Holland v Italy, 2008
008 **Matt Le Tissier**, Southampton v Newcastle, 1993
009 **Glenn Hoddle**, Tottenham v Manchester Utd, 1979
010 **Georgi Kinkladze**, Manchester City v Southampton, 1996
011 **Darío Rodríguez**, Uruguay v Denmark, 2002
012 **Leon Osman**, Everton v Larissa, 2007
013 **Eddie Gray**, Leeds v Burnley, 1970
014 **George Weah**, AC Milan v Verona, 1996
015 **Patrik Berger**, Charlton v Portsmouth, 2004
016 **Dennis Bergkamp**, Holland v Argentina, 1998
017 **Terry McDermott**, Tottenham Hotspur v Liverpool, 1980
018 **Wayne Rooney**, Everton v Arsenal, 2002
019 **Ricardo Fuller**, West Ham v Stoke, 2010
020 **John Harkes**, Derby v Sheffield Wednesday, 1990
021 **Chris Nicholl**, Aston Villa v Everton, 1977
022 **Lionel Messi**, Barcelona v Panathinaikos, 2010
023 **Trevor Sinclair**, QPR v Barnsley, 1997
024 **Bobby Charlton**, England v Mexico, 1966
025 **Lilian Nalis**, Leicester v Leeds, 2003
026 **John Barnes**, Brazil v England, June 1984
027 **Glen Johnson**, Portsmouth v Hull, 2008
028 **Henrik Larsson**, Sweden v Bulgaria, 2004
029 **Tony Yeboah**, Wimbledon v Leeds, 1995
030 **Cristiano Ronaldo**, Manchester Utd v Portsmouth, 2008
031 **Saeed Al-Owairan**, Saudi Arabia v Belgium, 1994
032 **Shaun Bartlett,** Charlton v Leicester, 2001
033 **Stephen Carr**, Tottenham v Sunderland, 2000
034 **Ashley Cole**, Chelsea v Sunderland, 2010
035 **Archie Gemmill**, Scotland v Holland, 1978
036 **Thierry Henry**, Arsenal v Manchester Utd, 2000
037 **Roy Wegerle**, Leeds v QPR, 1990
038 **Rivaldo**, Barcelona v Valencia, 2001
039 **Marco van Basten**, Holland v USSR, 1988
040 **Andrés D'Alessandro**, Portsmouth v Charlton, 2006
041 **Carlton Cole**, West Ham v Wigan, 2009
042 **Jon Harley**, Fulham v Aston Villa, 2003
043 **Mauro Bressan**, Fiorentina v Barcelona, 1999
044 **George Best**, Manchester Utd v Sheffield Utd, 1971
045 **Juliano Belletti,** Wigan v Chelsea, 2007
046 **Ernie Hunt**, Coventry v Everton, 1970
047 **Gareth Bale**, Inter v Tottenham, 2010

048 **Justin Fashanu**, Norwich v Liverpool, 1980
049 **Frank Worthington**, Bolton v Ipswich, 1979
050 **Thierry Henry**, Arsenal v Charlton, 2004
051 **Peter Crouch**, Liverpool v Galatasaray, 2006
052 **Denis Irwin**, Wimbledon v Manchester Utd, 1994
053 **Maynor Figueroa**, Stoke v Wigan, 2009
054 **Paolo Di Canio,** West Ham v Wimbledon, 2000
055 **Matt Taylor**, Portsmouth v Everton, 2006
056 **Diego Maradona**, Argentina v England, 1986
057 **Paul Gascoigne**, Tottenham v Arsenal, 1991
058 **Francis Lee**, Manchester City v Derby, 1974
059 **Kaká**, AC Milan v Fenerbahçe, 2005
060 **Wayne Rooney**, Manchester Utd v Newcastle, 2005
061 **Gus Poyet**, Chelsea v Sunderland, 1999
062 **Robin van Persie**, Charlton Athletic v Arsenal, 2006
063 **Maniche**, Portugal v Holland, 2004
064 **Dalian Atkinson**, Wimbledon v Aston Villa, 1992
065 **Alan Mullery**, Fulham v Leicester, 1974
066 **Steven Gerrard**, Liverpool v West Ham, 2006
067 **Esteban Cambiasso**,
    Argentina v Serbia & Montenegro, 2006
068 **Ryan Giggs**, Manchester Utd v Arsenal, 1999
069 **Alan Shearer**, Newcastle v Everton, 2002
070 **David Bentley**, Arsenal v Tottenham, 2008
071 **Roberto Baggio**, Italy v Czechoslovakia, 1990
072 **Daryl Murphy**, Sunderland v Wigan, 2008
073 **Gianfranco Zola**, Chelsea v Norwich, 2002

074 **Mick Channon**, Southampton v Liverpool, 1982
075 **Paul Gascoigne**, England v Scotland, 1996
076 **Zinedine Zidane**, Real Madrid v Bayer Leverkusen, 2002
077 **Cesc Fàbregas**, Arsenal v Tottenham, 2009
078 **Uwe Seeler**, West Germany v England, 1970
079 **Xabi Alonso**, Liverpool v Newcastle, 2006
080 **Lionel Messi**, Real Madrid v Barcelona, 2011
081 **Sebastian Larsson**, Tottenham v Birmingham, 2007
082 **David Beckham**, Wimbledon v Manchester Utd, 1996
083 **Ronnie Whelan**, Ireland v USSR, 1988
084 **Zlatan Ibrahimović**, Ajax v Breda, 2004
085 **David Ginola**, Barnsley v Tottenham, 1999
086 **Kanu**, Chelsea v Arsenal, 1999
087 **Pelé**, Brazil v Mexico, 1962
088 **Wayne Rooney**, Manchester Utd v Manchester City, 2011
089 **Nayim**, Real Zaragoza v Arsenal, 1995
090 **Matt Le Tissier**, Blackburn v Southampton, 1994
091 **Dejan Savićević**, AC Milan v Barcelona, 1994
092 **Ronnie Radford**, Hereford v Newcastle, 1972
093 **Mario Stanić**, Chelsea v West Ham, 2000
094 **Diego Maradona**, Argentina v Greece, 1994
095 **Steven Reid**, Wigan v Blackburn, 2005
096 **Ian Wright**, Wimbledon v Crystal Palace, 1991
097 **Ricky Villa**, Tottenham v Manchester City, 1981
098 **Trevor Sinclair**, West Ham v Derby, 2001
099 **Dennis Bergkamp**, Newcastle v Arsenal, 2002
100 **Michael Owen**, England v Argentina, 1998

Published by Yellow Jersey Press 2012
2 4 6 8 10 9 7 5 3 1

First published in Great Britain in 2012 by
Yellow Jersey Press
Random House, 20 Vauxhall Bridge Road,
London SW1V 2SA

www.randomhouse.co.uk

Addresses for companies within The Random House Group Limited can be found at: www.randomhouse.co.uk/offices.htm

The Random House Group Limited Reg. No. 954009

A CIP catalogue record for this book is available from the British Library

ISBN 978 0 22 409160 2

The Random House Group Limited supports The Forest Stewardship Council®(FSC®), the leading international forest certification organisation.
Our books carrying the FSC label are printed on FSC® certified paper. FSC is the only forest certification scheme endorsed by the leading
environmental organisations, including Greenpeace. Our paper procurement policy can be found at www.randomhouse.co.uk/environment

Page design by Doug Cheeseman
Printed and bound in China by C&C Offset Printing Co. Ltd..

Ex Libris